·EXPLORING·

THE VINEYARDS OF FRANCE

JULIAN WORTHINGTON

AN OWL BOOK

HENRY HOLT AND COMPANY
NEW YORK

Dedicated to André Fabry –
a charming and intrepid guide

Devised and produced by Templar Publishing Ltd.

Published in the United States by
Henry Holt and Company, Inc., 521 Fifth Avenue,
New York, New York 10175.

Library of Congress Cataloging-in-Publication Data
Worthington, Julian.
Exploring the vineyards of France
"An Owl book"
Includes index
1. Wine and wine making—France. I. Title.
TP553.W67   1987   663'.22'0944   87–8510
ISBN 0-8050-0446-7

First American Edition

Edited by Nicholas Bellenberg
Designed by Mick McCarthy
Color separations by Positive Colour Ltd.
Printed in Great Britain by Purnell Book Production Ltd.

10   9   8   7   6   5   4   3   2   1

ISBN 0-8050-0446-7

CONTENTS

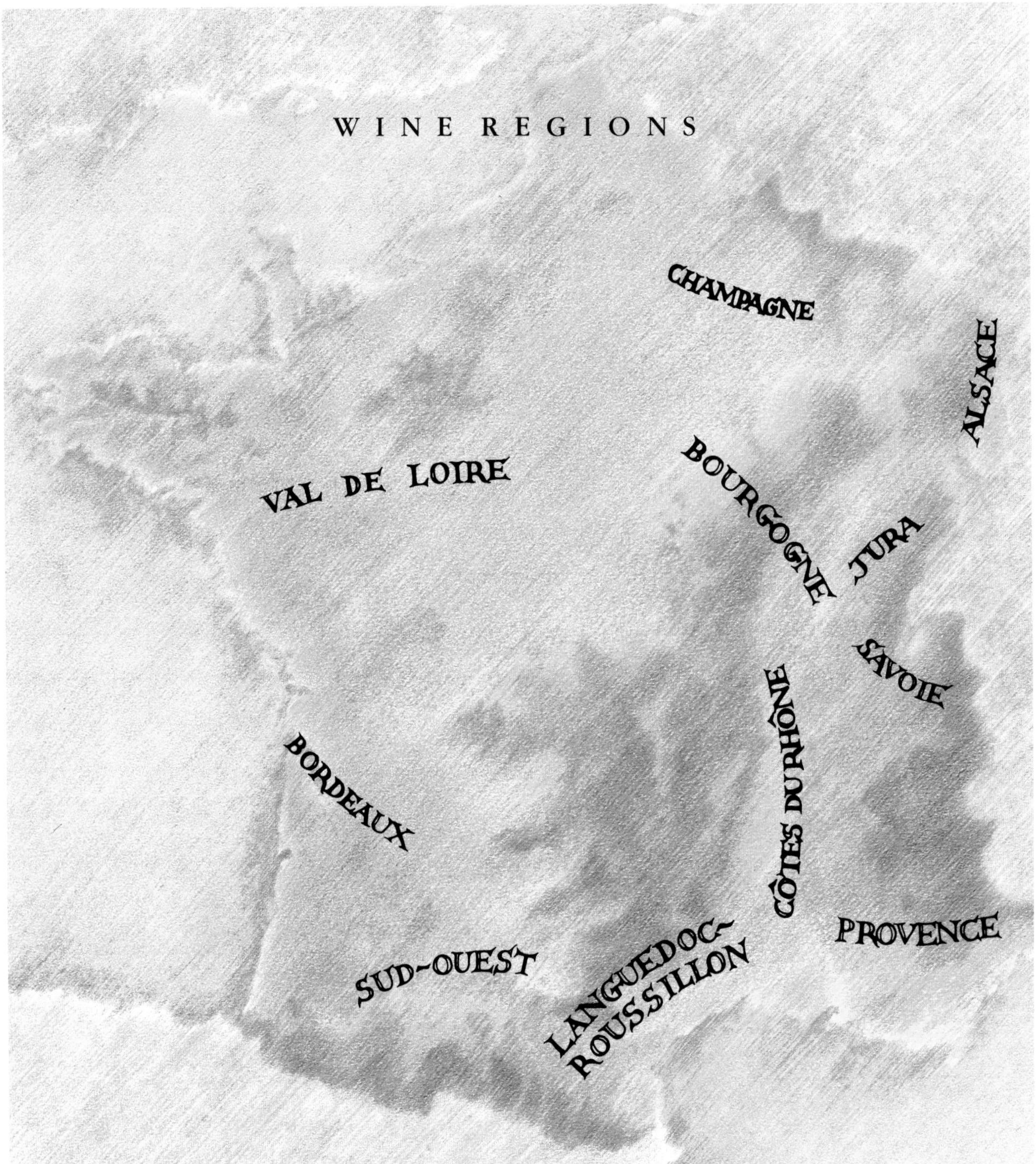

WINE REGIONS

CHAMPAGNE

ALSACE

VAL DE LOIRE

BOURGOGNE

JURA

SAVOIE

BORDEAUX

CÔTES DU RHÔNE

PROVENCE

SUD-OUEST

LANGUEDOC-ROUSSILLON

ESSENTIAL VINEYARD FRENCH

barrique	– hogshead/barrel	dégustation	– wine tasting	propriétaire	– owner
cave/caveau	– cellar	domaine	– estate	raisin	– grape
cèpage	– variety of grape	foudre	– wooden cask	salle de	
chai	– wine store	maison du vin	– literally "house of	dégustation	– tasting room
cuvaison	– fermentation of		wine"	santé	– your health!
	wine	méthode		terroir	– ground/soil
cuve	– fermentation vat	champenoise	– process by which	vendange	– harvest
cuvée	– vatful of wine		champagne and	vigne	– wine
cuvier	– vat room		other high quality	vigneron	– wine grower
dégorgement	– disgorgement of		sparkling wines are	vignoble	– vineyard
	sediment from		made	viticulteur	– wine grower
	méthode	millésieme	– vintage		
	champenoise	négociant	– wine trader		
	wines	pressoir	– wine press		

INTRODUCTION

There is a sign over a doorway in the winery at Château de Nouvelles, near Tuchan, in the region of Corbières, which reads: "A meal without wine is like a day without sun". Though we may be quite used to both conditions, one of the great pleasures to be gained from the French way of life is its cuisine, accompanied, naturally enough, by a glass or two of wine.

Through much of central and southern France vineyards flourish in some of the country's loveliest – and most spectacular – landscapes.

No visit to this part of the country would be complete without a taste of the wine and a look at where, and how, it is produced in all its rich variety. This then is the *raison d'être* for my guide to the vineyards of France – to help the visitor discover this variety and some of the people who dedicate their lives to the noble art of winemaking.

The vineyards have not been selected purely for the quality of their wines, although the choice offers a variety that I hope people of all tastes will enjoy. They have been chosen as examples of the many different situations and techniques under which French wines are produced.

You will find some of the grand châteaux in the guide, alongside much smaller *domaines* where wine production is carried out by small family units tending just a few hectares of vines. But all the vineyards included here have one very important aspect in common. They offer a warm and friendly welcome to the visitor, and are run by *vignerons* who will happily explain about their life and work. You should, however, remember that for the *vignerons* wine-making is a business. While they will normally welcome the opportunity of showing you around, they also have much work to do. So, be patient. When arranging a visit, it is best to 'phone first to make an appointment. Although not always necessary, it can save misunderstandings and wasted journeys.

As a general rule, vineyards are open for visiting during the week from 8 am until 6 pm and often later, allowing a break for lunch between 12 and 2 pm. Some will be open at the weekend, too. Although most *vignerons* will try to accommodate you during the *vendange*, which is carried out during October and in some areas through into early November, be prepared for the occasional disappointment as some vineyards close their doors during this busy harvest time.

The visitor should try to speak and understand the native tongue. Generally, most *vignerons* are tolerant and patient, and you will find greater respect and a better response if you are prepared to struggle with the language.

Buying wines from the places you visit will probably be one object of your trip. Certainly recalling the vineyard and the people who made the wine adds an extra savour to the vintage upon returning home – supposing it lasts that long! This guide also offers some background on wine-making in France, and the practicalities of buying wine abroad.

Many vineyards have leaflets for visitors and other information about their wine and that of the area. Each region also has a trade organisation, normally called a *Comité Interprofessionel*, where you can get much more general information and often details of wine routes through the area. The addresses and telephone numbers of these bodies are included in the guide. And don't forget the *Offices de Tourisme* or *Syndicats d'Initiative*, which you should find in all major towns. The people there are usually very helpful and willing to point you in the right direction. There are *Maisons du Vin* in some of the larger, more important wine areas which can be very useful too.

I hope those of you who use this guide gain as much enjoyment as I did in its preparation. To the fine *vignerons* and all the other friends I made during my travels – and to you, the reader – *Santé!*

Marden, Kent

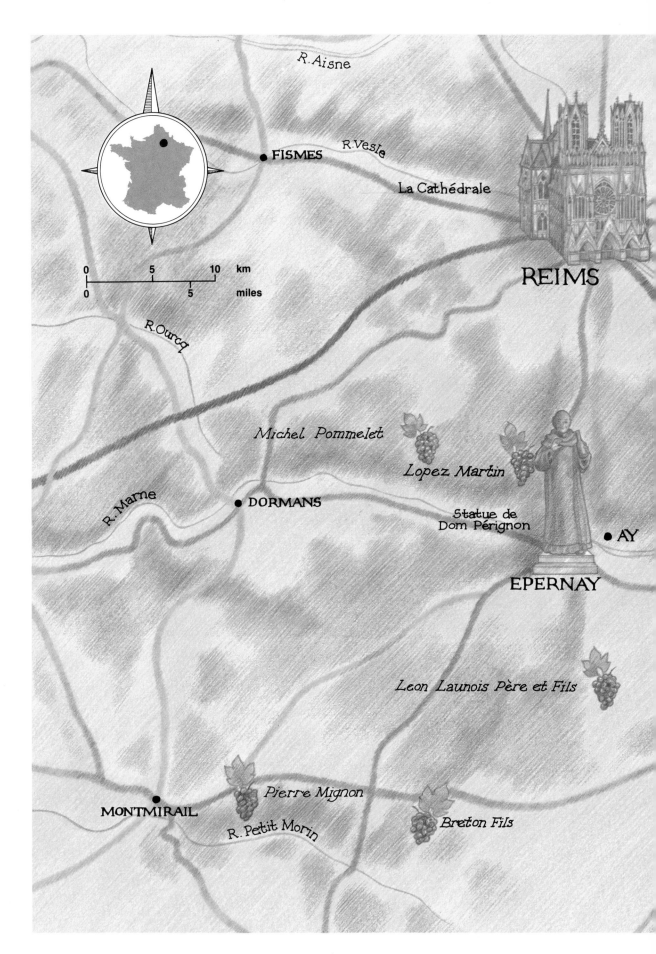

R. Aisne

FISMES

R. Vesle

La Cathédrale

REIMS

R. Ourcq

Michel Pommelet

Lopez Martin

R. Marne

DORMANS

Statue de
Dom Pérignon

AY

EPERNAY

Leon Launois Père et Fils

Pierre Mignon

MONTMIRAIL

R. Petit Morin

Breton Fils

0   5   10   km
0   5   miles

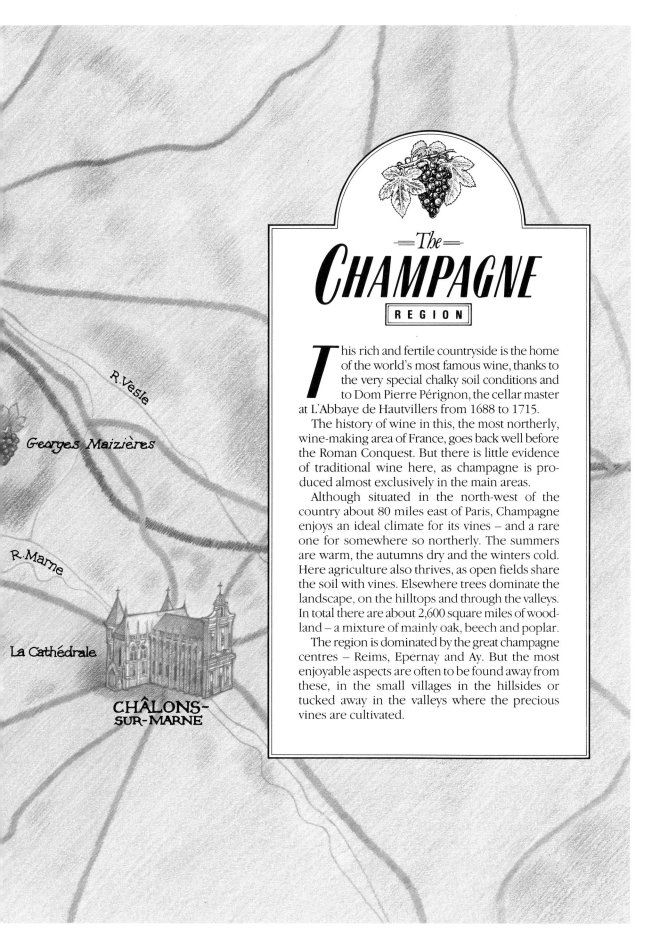

R.Vesle

Georges Maizières

R.Marne

La Cathédrale

CHÂLONS-
SUR-MARNE

The CHAMPAGNE
REGION

This rich and fertile countryside is the home of the world's most famous wine, thanks to the very special chalky soil conditions and to Dom Pierre Pérignon, the cellar master at L'Abbaye de Hautvillers from 1688 to 1715.

The history of wine in this, the most northerly, wine-making area of France, goes back well before the Roman Conquest. But there is little evidence of traditional wine here, as champagne is produced almost exclusively in the main areas.

Although situated in the north-west of the country about 80 miles east of Paris, Champagne enjoys an ideal climate for its vines – and a rare one for somewhere so northerly. The summers are warm, the autumns dry and the winters cold. Here agriculture also thrives, as open fields share the soil with vines. Elsewhere trees dominate the landscape, on the hilltops and through the valleys. In total there are about 2,600 square miles of woodland – a mixture of mainly oak, beech and poplar.

The region is dominated by the great champagne centres – Reims, Epernay and Ay. But the most enjoyable aspects are often to be found away from these, in the small villages in the hillsides or tucked away in the valleys where the precious vines are cultivated.

The
CHAMPAGNE
REGION

Champagne's wine is famous throughout the world, but perhaps not so well known are the delightful country-side and peaceful villages on which the region's international success is founded. Several routes offer the visitor hours of enjoyment and pleasure. These cover the main vine-growing sectors of Champagne – Montagne de Reims, Vallée de la Marne, Côte des Blancs and the region of L'Aube, to be found to the south.

Reims is the champagne capital. The mighty cathedral takes pride of place in the city, for it was here that most of the kings of France were consecrated. Other highlights include the Porte Mars, the Gallo-Roman forum and several fascinating museums and churches.

Around Reims, particularly to the south – bordering the celebrated forests, are some of the finest vineyards. The valleys of the Adre and Vesle rivers provide most picturesque settings for walking, amid villages with fine churches and much rustic charm. Passing through Gueux and Ville-Dommange, with its vast panorama, you will come to Verzenay, where there is a windmill, visible from far away. Continuing on this route you come to Verzy, with its forest of strange twisted beech trees.

Travelling south from Verzy via Trépail and the delight-fully named town of Bouzy, you can move on to the area which is the traditional home of champagne – Ay – and its capital Epernay. Like Reims, this town boasts great and well-known champagne houses. But all around the area, the villages are full of excellent smaller producers busy making the unique sparkling wine. From Epernay,

you should make the pilgrimage to Hautvillers, a charming spot on the hillside overlooking the Marne, where the famed Dom Pérignon perfected the famous blending process some 300 years ago.

Further to the south from Hautvillers lies the Côte des Blancs, where only white grapes are used to make champagne. The wine route takes you through the rolling chalky countryside so typical of this area, past Cramant, Avize, Oger and on to Vertus. To the west of Epernay, as the road takes you on towards Château Thierry, you follow the course of the Marne along a green and fertile valley with vineyards spread mainly along the right bank.

Heading through the thickly wooded hillsides south of the Marne, you come to the smaller vineyards of the Petite Vallée de la Marne, passing through charming rural hamlets with their traditional grey stone houses. There is a magnificent abbey to visit at Orgbais, while Etoges boasts a 17th century château. Coizard-Joches is famous for its druid stones, grottoes and caves.

Near the captivating town of Troyes, with its narrow streets of wooden houses – rich in museums and churches – are the outlying vineyards of L'Aube. The valleys are dotted with pleasant villages like Essoyes, Les Riceys and Mussy-sur-Seine around Bar-sur-Seine which has an interesting church and picturesque ancient streets. Close by Bar-sur-Aube you can enjoy the green fertile landscape around Arrentieres and Arconville. And for the final pilgrimage, there is the tomb of General Charles de Gaulle at Colombey-les-Deux-Eglises.

REGIONAL SPECIALITIES

The Wines
Champagne is unique, and no other sparkling wine can be given its name. Only wines produced in Champagne, from grapes grown in the area's vineyards qualify. Pink champagne is made in small quantities, but many vineyards look upon it as a novelty. However, there are other local wines. Some excellent still whites are produced – called Coteaux Champenois – as well as some reds – Bouzy for instance – which some say do not travel well and are best enjoyed locally. The region is also known for its local beer.

The Food
The famous wine is not just for drinking, for here it is used in food as well, ecrevisse au Champagne (crayfish) and sabayon au Champagne (mousse) for example. Specialities include pig's trotters, particularly from Sainte-Menehould, and gigue de chevreuil des Ardennes (haunch of venison with baked apples). If you enjoy fish, there is truite (trout) à la crème, while split pea purée makes an interesting dish. Try the cheeses too – such as Chaource or Langres.

Above. Surrounded by the ripe autumn vines, the wine-making village of Oger is set in the heart of the Côte des Blancs.
Far left. Champagne casks rest in grand surroundings.
Left. Father of a legend, Dom Pierre Pérignon perfected the technique of blending champagne and controlling the secondary fermentation in the 17th century.

MICHEL POMMELET

F L E U R Y · L A · R I V I E R E

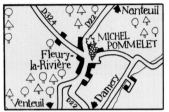

The small village of Fleury-la-Rivière lies just to the north of the Marne, on the hillsides that form part of the important champagne-producing valley west of Epernay. Its people have worked with the vines for generations, and most of their produce is handled by the *co-opérative* at the south end of the village.

There is, however, a handful of independent growers who produce and bottle their own champagne. One of these is Michel Pommelet, a neat, reticent, but very polite *vigneron* who speaks modestly about himself, his family and his business. Here you will probably see the greatest contrast to the grand champagne production centres.

With the full support of his family – and particularly his eldest son Christophe – M. Pommelet looks after just 3 hectares of vines and produces about 20,000 bottles each year. His winery contains the basic essentials for making champagne and there are few frills. The bottles are turned by hand and M. Pommelet or his son also carries out the *dégorgement* (removal of the wine's sediment).

Coming from a family that boasts three generations of vine-growers, M. Pommelet is as refreshing as the sparkling

wine he produces. As you settle down in the family's homely front room to taste the delightful results of the Pommelets' endeavours, you have to warm to the sincerity and modesty of this dedicated *vigneron*.

Looking out from M. Pommelet's property across the vineyards towards the Marne, it is easy to understand why families like the Pommelets devote their life to the production of wine – and the speciality known as champagne.

Michel Pommelet
5 Rue des Long Champs
Fleury-la-Rivière
51200 Epernay
Telephone: 26 58 41 04

Most champagne is a blend of red and white grapes. The main varieties used are Chardonnay (**above**), Meunier and Pinot Noir (**above right**).

LOPEZ-MARTIN

H A U T V I L L E R S

Hautvillers – a charming late 18th century property.

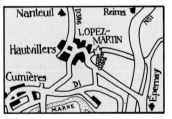

No tour around the Champagne region would be complete without a pilgrimage to the village where it all began about 300 years ago when Dom Pérignon, the abbey's cellarmaster, discovered the method of making sparkling wine.

But Hautvillers has more to offer than sentiment. The village itself is quite delightful, with its narrow streets and ancient houses. Perched up on high ground above Epernay, it also commands a magnificent view across the Vallée de la Marne, and the precious vineyards spread down from the tree-topped hill of the Montagne de Reims.

Among the wine-producers in Hautvillers, you will find the Lopez family hard at work in their cave, down the road from the village below the family home. The house itself has an arched entrance leading into a pleasant courtyard. Four generations of *viticulteurs* have produced champagne from here since the turn of the century.

The reason why the *cave* is some distance from the house is quite simple. The property, according to the stone above the entrance, was built in 1797 just after the French Revolution. It was originally a farmhouse and had no need of a cellar. When great-grandfather Lopez bought the house and wanted to make wine, he had to look for suitable facilities. At the bottom of the hill he found a set of cellars that were ideal for a *cave*, since they had previously been used for just that purpose by the monks from the abbey. They had been carved out of the rock by the monks themselves some 250 years ago and are some of the oldest in the village.

Above left. *The labour-intensive nature of champagne production is obvious at Hautvillers. The distinctive mushroom corks are inserted with a corking machine.*
Above. *Removing the secondary fermentation's sediment – the* dégorgement – *is wet work, as Pierre Lopez demonstrates.*

There's a lot to enjoy here – particularly the traditional vaulted cellars, where the precious champagne is kept in its bottles until the *dégorgement*. Pierre Lopez carries this out deftly by hand – at a rate of some 250/300 bottles per hour. Above all, you will receive a welcome as genuine as the wine produced from this, the historical birthplace of champagne.

Lopez-Martin *(Pierre & Patrick Lopez)*
Les Côtes de l'Hery
Hautvillers
51160 Ay
Telephone: 26 59 42 17

GEORGES MAIZIERES
T R E P A I L

On a high bank, Champagne's Chardonnay vines ripen in the summer sun.

One of the main champagne producing areas – the Montagne de Reims – includes the sloping ground on the south side of the thick forest that separates Epernay and Reims. To the north-east is the appropriately named village of Bouzy, and beyond lies Trépail, tucked into the hillside below the tree-topped "mountains".

At the far end of the village, next to the sports field which is cut into the hills, is the home and winery of the Maizières family. George Maizières relies heavily on help from his wife Eveline and daughter Sylvie, to ensure that the business runs smoothly and efficiently.

By normal standards, this is a modest concern, since George Maizières has just 5 hectares of vines – three around the village, one on the other side of the hill at Bouilly and one nearby at Bouzy. At the Bouzy vineyard he grows Pinot Noir, from which a red wine is made, just to add a little variety to the range of champagne.

M. Maizières claims to be a descendant of one of the oldest families in the area – if not the region. He can trace the family name back to 1599. The name "Georges Maizières" has been used uninterrupted through all the male generations. The present business was set up here in 1973, since when it has gone from strength to strength – particularly after 1982 when full production was achieved.

There's plenty of interest to see in this "new" winery, with a three-tiered cave that goes down some 13 metres. It is also good to see that, despite the modern production facilities, M. Maizières still believes in using wood to store the wine. His Blanc de Blancs and Millésime vintages are kept for a time in oak before being bottled.

One curious and potentially useful feature is a small but well-equipped apartment (or *gîte*) alongside the winery. This can be used by visitors who wish to extend their stay – or simply for those who need to retire for a while, having sampled a little too much of the vineyard's wonderful offerings!

Georges Maizières
1 Rue du Stade
Trépail
51150 Tours-sur-Marne
Telephone: 26 57 05 04

LEON LAUNOIS PERE et FILS
LE MESNIL - SUR - OGER

Left. *The 18th century house of Leon Launois, basking in the autumn sunshine.*
Above. *One of the Launois' huge presses stands ready and waiting for action.*

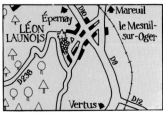

Tucked away up the narrow streets of Le Mesnil-sur-Oger, about 20 minutes' drive from the champagne centre at Epernay, is the house of Léon Launois, which has produced some excellent Blanc de Blancs for the best part of this century.

This elegant urban property with its large courtyard, entered through a narrow archway, was founded in the early part of the 18th century. Here the Launois family has tended its vineyard and produced wine through successive generations ever since. Léon and his son Jacques currently run 18 hectares of vines, 12 of which are spread round the village itself.

Jacques handles the general running of this relatively modest business very professionally, showing visitors round the winery and looking after clients – of which there is now an impressive selection. The business has been built up over the years since his grandfather started exploiting the champagne market and production now averages 100,000 bottles a year.

There are plenty of interesting aspects at the winery at Le Mesnil to admire; such as the two traditional 4000 kilo presses the split-level *cave*, buried deep underground and linked to the surface by a lift. One fascinating aspect for the more technically minded, is the set of *pupitres*, which hold the champagne bottles and turn them automatically to ensure that the sediment settles in the bottles' necks before *dégorgement*.

Naturally, the grapes have to be carefully chosen in the first place and this means that throughout the region the *vendange* is carried out by hand. Here at Le Mesnil up to 100 people are brought in to pick the Launois' grapes, to ensure the harvest takes the minimum amount of time – usually about seven or eight days.

After visiting the winery, where you can gain a good understanding of the different stages of production involved in this particular side of wine-making, you can relax in the comfortable reception room and quietly sip the results of at least four years of care and attention – an excellent glass of Côte des Blancs champagne, a refreshing and delightful experience to end your visit.

Léon Launois Père et Fils
3 Ruelle de l'Arquebuse
Le Mesnil-sur-Oger
51190 Avize
Telephone: 26 57 50 28

BRETON FILS
C O N G Y

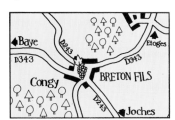

Few trips to the vineyards of Champagne will give you more pleasure than a drive through the Côte des Blancs to one of the outposts of the region – the house of Breton Fils in the small village of Congy. Here you are assured of a genuine family welcome, since father, mother, son and daughter-in-law are all involved in the day-to-day running of this modest, but fascinating vineyard.

By local standards the enterprise is a young one, started in 1945, when Inge and Olivette Breton produced the princely sum of 300 bottles. Since then, through gradual purchase, development and expansion, the property has grown. Today the Bretons can boast a production of 100,000 bottles a year, from the 15 hectares of vines spread round the countryside at Ay, Sezanne, Férebrianges and Etopes, as well as Congy.

Alongside the family members, two other people are employed during the year, with about 60 extra hands during the *vendange*.

The fruits of their labour, some 300,000 bottles at any one time, are stored in various parts of the winery – including the maze of tunnels that makes up the deep cellars. You enter the cellars down a long series of stone steps from just inside the front room. The traditional

Bottles of champagne are set in these pupitres *in Breton Fils' caves, to allow the sediment in the wine to settle in the necks prior to the* dégorgement.

champagne cellars have been hand-hewn from the stone by M. Breton and his son over the last 30 years – and they haven't finished yet.

There's an easier way up through the floors that house more stored bottles, since a lift connects the various areas of production. Traditional methods are still adopted here, even down to the *dégorgement*, which Inge Breton still carries out by hand, as he is happy to demonstrate.

Breton Fils (Inge Breton)
12 Rue Courte-Pilate
Congy
51270 Montmort
Telephone: 26 59 31 03

PIERRE MIGNON
L E   B R E U I L

Although Le Breuil is situated in one of the most southerly vine-growing parts of the Champagne region, the trip there is an excursion well worth taking. You'll be some way off the main "wine route" along the Vallée de la Marne and you'll pass through some rich, changing countryside, which at times opens out into a vista of rolling hills, then closes in to thick woodland.

Le Breuil is a quiet, friendly village tucked in the folds of the hillside that make up part of the "Petite Vallée de la Marne". Standing on rising ground overlooking the rest of the community is the home and winery of the Mignon family, appropriately situated in Rue des Grappes d'Or.

Here you can expect a friendly welcome from either

Top. *The village of Damery, situated on the north bank of the Marne, near Epernay.*
Above. *A Champagne cellarman carries out the remauge –* twisting the bottles *in the* pupitres *to encourage the sediment to settle.*

production has been centred around champagne.

An average of 100,000 bottles is the result of the harvest from the Mignons' 8 hectares of vines, along with other grapes they buy in. With a well-equipped winery, the Mignons also offer their facilities to other smaller growers in the commune and each year press their grapes as well.

One of the most interesting features the visitor can enjoy came about completely by accident. Several years ago work had just started on extending the chai and a bulldozer was hired to excavate some of the land. During the operation a small arched entrance with a gaping hole in the ground was uncovered. The driver stopped just in time and immediately told M. Mignon. Further investigation revealed part of a ready-made cellar, which could well have been used as a store area by the occupants of the old abbey on the hill above.

Work is currently going on to extend these fascinating cellars, to provide the traditional type of storage for champagne. They will certainly prove an important feature of this friendly, family vineyard.

Pierre Mignon or his charming wife Yveline. They will chat knowledgeably about the vineyard and the wine, and take you around this well-organised, workmanlike property. Wine has been made here by the same family since about 1860, although it is only in the last 40 years or so that

Pierre Mignon
Rue des Grappes d'Or
Le Breuil
51210 Montmirail
Telephone: 26 59 22 03

TYPES OF GRAPE

*T*he wine vine, *Vitis Vinifera*, is only one of a huge family of plants which includes as many as 5,000 varieties. Of these only some 50 are used to grow grapes for wine.

The basic difference in the taste of a wine depends on the type of grape from which it is made. If you are able to distinguish the major grape varieties, you will have a better idea of what wines you're going to like before you buy.

In France's traditional wine producing regions the grape varieties best suited to the local soil and climate have been selected over many centuries. These now combine the highest quality, linked with factors such as yield and resistance to disease.

In many places no one grape can provide exactly what is needed, and the wine is a result of the blending of several types. In others the wine is traditionally, and often in *law*, made from a single variety. White burgundy, for example, has to be made solely from Chardonnay grapes and its red counterpart from the Pinot Noir variety.

The degree of flavour a particular grape variety produces depends to a large extent upon the quantity of fruit each vine carries. In most cases the larger the grape yield is in relation to the unit area of the vineyard, the less flavour the final wine is likely to have. This means that the larger-yielding, modern hybrid vines are often banned from the Appellation Contrôlée wine areas.

As the wine world has become more "variety conscious" newer wine-producing countries, particularly Australia and the USA, have tended to feature the varietal name prominently on the bottle label. Germany, too, follows this practice. But in France – with the exception of Germany's close neighbour Alsace – the long tradition of wine making means that it is accepted which varieties go into which wines. Naming the grape variety on the label is, therefore, considered "unnecessary" in France.

WHITE WINE GRAPES

Chardonnay
The grape used to produce white burgundy and champagne. Provides dry white wine of great complexity.

Riesling
The classic grape of Germany. True Riesling is also grown in Alsace where it is made into drier wine than over the border.

Chenin Blanc
The main grape of the middle Loire (Vouvray, Layon etc). Can be dry or sweet, but its high acidity means it ages well.

Sémillon
Gives the lusciousness to Sauternes by having the ability to "rot nobly" on the vine. This concentrates the grape's sugar content.

Muscat
The easiest variety to distinguish as it smells and tastes of grapes! Mostly made into perfumed sweet wine.

Sauvignon Blanc
Has a very distinctive steely dry flavour (as in Pouilly Fumé). Used blended with Semillon in Bordeaux.

Aligoté
Burgundy's everyday grape. Makes crisp wine, but needs drinking young.

Muscadet
Used to make light, very dry wines around the mouth of the Loire.

Pinot Blanc
A near relation of Chardonnay. Grown in the same areas, but having less character.

RED WINE GRAPES

Carignan
By far the commonest grape of France. Prolific but dull.

Merlot
Blended with Cabernet Sauvignon to produce soft fruity wines.

Grenache
A sweet grape used in a blend to make Châteauneuf-du-Pape and Tavel Rosé.

Cabernet Franc
Second grape of Bordeaux, also used for red Loires, with an aroma often reminiscent of raspberries.

Syrah
The best red grape of the Rhône making dark, long-lived wine.

Cabernet Sauvignon
Gives a long-lasting wine, tough when young but ageing superbly. It is the main grape of red Bordeaux (claret), though always blended (usually with Merlot).

Gamay
The fresh and fruity grape at its best in Beaujolais.

Pinot Noir
Classic red burgundy grape and an important ingredient in Champagne where it is vinified off (without) the skins to produce white wine.

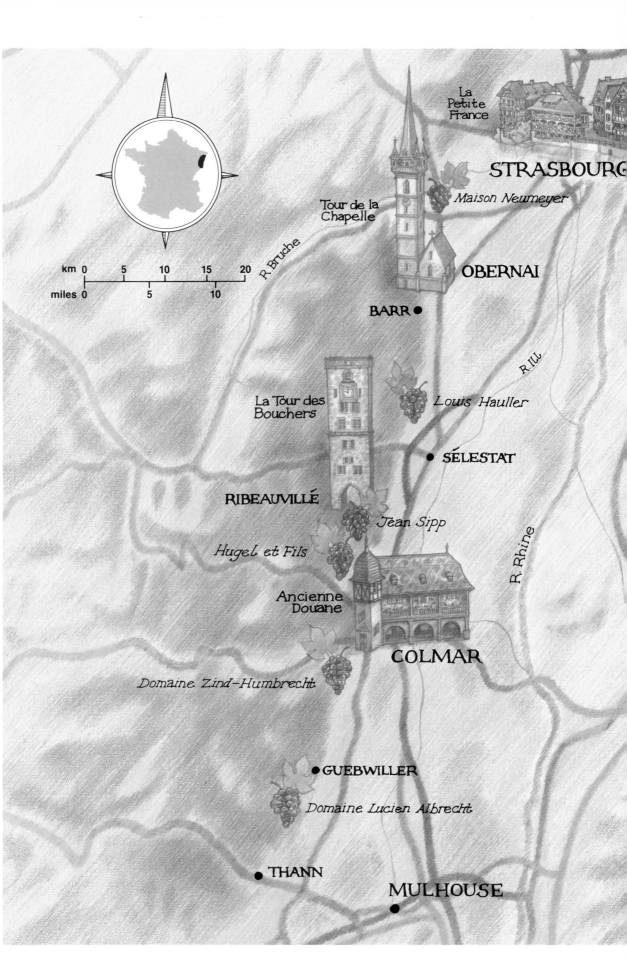

La Petite
France

STRASBOURG

Tour de la
Chapelle

Maison Neumeyer

OBERNAI

R. Bruche

BARR •

km 0   5   10   15   20
miles 0   5   10

La Tour des
Bouchers

Louis Hauller

R. Ill

• SÉLESTAT

RIBEAUVILLÉ

Jean Sipp

Hugel et Fils

R. Rhine

Ancienne
Douane

COLMAR

Domaine Zind-Humbrecht

• GUEBWILLER

Domaine Lucien Albrecht

• THANN

MULHOUSE
•

The ALSACE

REGION

One of France's most northerly wine regions, Alsace stretches along the foothills of the Vosges mountains for about 80 miles between Strasbourg and Mulhouse.

Historically, the area has suffered something of an identity crisis, through the turmoil and changes of many wars that have left it with mainly German place names, but a population that is fervently French. Certainly the success of the wine industry is a tribute to the resilience and courage of its people.

Travelling through the region of Alsace, from Strasbourg in the north following the course of the Rhine to Thann and Mulhouse in the south, is like a trip through fairyland. There is a magical charm about these towns and villages tucked into the foothills of the Vosges mountains that leaves you breathless.

Alsace is like nowhere else in France. Indeed, but for the language, you could be forgiven for believing that the German border was to the west and not to the east of this fascinating region, where the typical dry, white, fruity wines complement the generally excellent cuisine.

The ALSACE
REGION

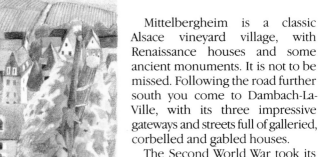

The countryside of Alsace is at times spectacular, with its mixture of dark pine forests and mountain pastures along the slopes of the Vosges, opening out into expansive plains that spread along both sides of the Rhine. The main centres of population and commerce have developed on these plains – Strasbourg, Colmar and Mulhouse being the most significant.

These large towns provide a stark contrast to the fortified villages that are at the heart of the region's wine-making. As you travel through the impressive gateways and along the quaint cobbled streets of these villages, you'll pass many tall, gabled, Renaissance houses – built when many wine merchants made quick fortunes.

Near to Strasbourg is the historic town of Marlenheim. From Nordheim, with its splendid flower-decked Alsatian houses, you can enjoy a magnificent view over the plain of Alsace and Strasbourg. Continuing south, well worth visiting is the delightful village of Sainte-les-Bains, tucked away in the Mossig valley. Also interesting is the ancient village of Dangolsheim, built more than 1000 feet up on the hillside.

Moving south, the university and cathedral city of Molsheim is found amid countryside of vineyards and orchards. Passing through the historic towns of Boersch and Obernai you reach the spectacular religious monument of Sainte Odile, over 2000 feet up in the mountains above the pine forests.

Mittelbergheim is a classic Alsace vineyard village, with Renaissance houses and some ancient monuments. It is not to be missed. Following the road further south you come to Dambach-La-Ville, with its three impressive gateways and streets full of galleried, corbelled and gabled houses.

The Second World War took its toll of many of the villages in this area. Of those that survived relatively unscathed, Ribeauvillé, overlooked by the Three Castles of Ribeaupierre, is full of historical interest for the visitor. Other well preserved towns are Zellenberg, from which there are superb views, and Riquewihr, with its defensive gateways, cobbled streets and many fascinating houses – surely one of the finest French wine villages.

Turkheim is another fortified Alsatian town – traces of the town's walls are still visible. Some of the best vines in the region are grown on the slopes of the Hengst around Wintzenheim, while feudal castles (such as the one at Eguisheim) dominate the landscape and provide much local interest. East of Wintzenheim is the Alsace's wine capital Colmar. This picturesque old town is famed for its museum and library.

Following the wine route to the west of Colmar, you will sight the famous ruins of the Three Castles, overlooking a spectacular panorama that takes in the plains of Alsace. Further south lies the terraced village of Orschwihr, bordered by the Bollenberg and Pfingstberg-Lippelsberg hills.

REGIONAL SPECIALITIES

The Wines
Major types: *Sylvaner, Riesling, Gewurtztraminer, Muscat d'Alsace, Pinot Blanc (Klevner), Pinot Gris (Tokay d'Alsace), Pinot Noir (Rosé d'Alsace).*

The Food
Traditional food to be found in Alsatian restaurants inevitably includes onion tart, choucroute *(pickled cabbage with meat and sausage)* Coq au Riesling *and Munster cheese. You will find delicious variations on these basics, such as pheasant* choucroute *and Munster valley tart. Also look out for*

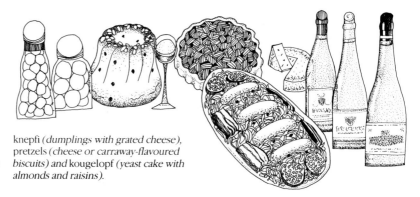

knepfi *(dumplings with grated cheese),* pretzels *(cheese or carraway-flavoured biscuits) and* kougelopf *(yeast cake with almonds and raisins).*

Top. A typical Alsatian scene – a vineyard during the vendange.
Above. Other crafts are carried out in the Alsace in addition to the important job of wine making.
Left. Le Rue des Tanneurs in Colmar, Alsace's wine capital.

MAISON NEUMEYER

MOLSHEIM

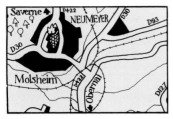

Lying at the foot of the Vosges range, to the northern end of the Alsace wine region, Molsheim is an ancient university and cathedral city. Records show that the church owned and cultivated vines as long ago as 822. The Neumeyers, with one or two other *vignerons*, have recently regenerated some of these ancient vineyards. They are again producing wine whose traditions go back more than 10 centuries.

Gerard Neumeyer talks knowledgeably about the history of the area's wine. He is proud to be producing once again the wine named by the 9th century monks and friars. There is, for example, the Finkenberg, which disappeared after the French Revolution. Now the Neumeyers have recreated a Riesling from the vines on that part of the hillside. There is also a Riesling and a Gerwurztraminer made from the Brunderthal vineyards, which once produced these wines in plenty.

If Gerard has the time he will happily explain this history and talk about the 13 hectares of vines the family owns and cultivates, and from where the pleasant selection of wine originates. Whether you're just looking round, sampling the wine, or interested in the local history, a trip to the Maison Neumeyer offers many rewards.

Maison Neumeyer (*Gerard Neumeyer*)
19 Rue du General-de-Gaulle
67120 Molsheim
Telephone: 88 38 12 45

High in the mountains south-west of Obernai is the convent founded in the 7th century by Alsace's patron, Sainte Odile.

LOUIS HAULLER

DAMBACH-LA-VILLE

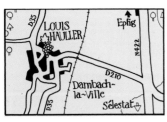

The 11th century Chapel of Saint Sebastian stands prominently on the hillside, guarding the walled town of Dambach-La-Ville. Close to the chapel is the house of Louis Hauller, whose family has produced wine since 1886.

The property itself goes back further. The inscription on the front wall says 1768 – and curiously the "1" and the "7" are the wrong way round. It is very much in the same style as other tall, gabled buildings in the maze of tiny streets that make up this typical Alsatian town.

The Haullers have always made and sold their own wines. However, in the atmospheric cellar just next door, M. Hauller has opened a tiny *caveau* displaying a selection

of wines from all the regions of France.

The cellar is largely the responsibility of Louis' wife, Marie-Thérèse Hauller, who is very much a working partner – not just here but also in the running of the 8 hectares of vines. A good range of wines is produced – including Sylvaner, Riesling, Tokay and Gerwurztraminer – which has over the years won the family many awards.

The wine cellar is most atmospheric, with antique wooden barrels lining both side walls. Most of these were made by the family. Mme Hauller has also started a display of wine artefacts. Whenever possible, she adds to this "mini museum" to make a point of extra interest for visitors.

Louis Hauller
92 Rue du Maréchal Foch
67650 Dambach-La-Ville
Telephone: 88 92 41 19

JEAN SIPP

R I B E A U V I L L E

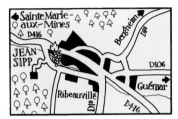

The house of the Sipp family, which is more than 400 years old, is built into the original city wall and was, for much of the time, the home of the nobles of Ribeauvillé.

The property is steeped in history, with the remains of one of the old round towers in the garden. Now sadly covered in foliage, the tower was once a prison. However, the Sipps have only been resident here this century. Since Jean Sipp bought the house, four generations have been involved in making wine – and, rather confusingly, all the men have been called Jean.

Looking after the 20 hectares of vines is very much a family business. At the time of our visit, son Jean was busy with his team of helpers ploughing up new land on the steep hillside above this ancient town, in order to plant more vines. The ground was so steep that the plough had to be powered by a motor-driven pulley to lift it up and through the soil that had lain barren for years.

Under the house is the *caveau*, full of interesting old wine-making equipment. Here in pleasant, comfortable surroundings you can sit and taste some of the 15 or so wines the Sipps produce. A member of the family will also take you round the winery, where traditional methods go hand-in-hand with some modern machinery.

You will find the Sipp's house at the top end of the town. At the bottom end, as you enter from the main road, is the property of a cousin and *négociant* Louis Sipp.

Jean Sipp
60 Rue de la Fraternité
68150 Ribeauvillé
Telephone: 89 73 60 02

Even helped by a winch, ploughing this barren land was still hard work for vigneron Jean Sipp.

HUGEL et FILS

R I Q U E W I H R

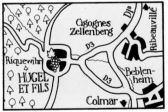

Riquewihr is a classic medieval Alsatian town, steeped in history with many fascinating places of interest. The fortifications, dating back to the 13th century, are well preserved. Inside the walls you discover a maze of cobbled streets lined with magnificent tall, gabled, Renaissance-styled buildings.

The house of Hugel et Fils stands proudly in the centre of Riquewihr, with a family history that goes back to the heydays of the 1600s, when the town flourished. Through

The house of Hugel et Fils in the medieval town of Riquewihr.

successive generations from 1639 to the present day, the Hugels have made wine.

The turning point in the family's modern-day fortunes came when, just after the 1914-18 war, grandfather Jean decided to concentrate on improving the quality of his wine. Until then the emphasis in the region was very much on quantity, but after the war, the *vignerons* had to look for new markets. It was Jean Hugel who led the way in this new challenge.

Thus, today, quality is strictly controlled here. For example, from the moment the harvest arrives, the juice from every container of grapes is tested and then colour-coded with a label.

The reputation of the Hugel wines has been gained through careful and dedicated management. Three brothers run the business – Georges, André and Jean. Very much the spokesman, Jean – or Johnny, as he has become known – is a lively, ebullient and very knowledgeable character. And he is emphatic when he says: "You cannot make a good wine in the cellar." In other words, it's very much down to the grapes.

There is plenty of interest to see at this family vineyard. The most impressive feature in the cellar is the "Saint Caterine cask" which dates from 1715. The Hugels proudly boast that it is the oldest still in use in France – probably in the world.

The network of cellars runs under several blocks of streets and each is connected underground by pipes that carry the wine to and from the main winery. This was the only option open to an expanding business run from medieval buildings. In all, there is a capacity for some two

A scene typical of Alsace, historical buildings and vineyards exist side-by-side in rural tranquility.

million litres of wine, the product of a range of grapes from not only the Hugel's own 25 hectares, but 110 hectares of other growers, whose harvest is bought each year.

The tasting area is in a low-vaulted room where, if you can persuade Johnny to officiate, you can enjoy a most rewarding experience.

Hugel et Fils
68340 Riquewihr
Telephone: 89 47 92 15

DOMAINE ZIND-HUMBRECHT
W I N T Z E N H E I M

Wood carving is very much an Alsatian craft, although not many people still wear these hand-made sabots or clogs.

The Humbrechts are one of the most well established families in the area, tracing their ancestry back to 1620 and the Thirty Years War. Sadly, no records exist prior to that date.

Ever since then the family tradition of wine production has been maintained. The business has its beginnings in nearby Guberschwihr, although it is only since 1947 that the Humbrechts have exclusively devoted themselves to making and selling their own wine. The Domaine itself was created in 1959 when the family pooled its resources with those of the Zinds of Wintzenheim.

The size of the vineyards, and the reputation of the wines produced, has grown enormously during this period. Now 30 hectares of vines go to make 25 different wines. The secret of the success of this partnership lies partly in the fact that traditional methods have been religiously retained.

Mechanisation has been kept to a minimum here – in the form of a pneumatic press. This uses an inflatable tube in a cylinder to gently press the grapes. The juice is then gravity-fed straight into wooden casks to ferment. They don't even use pumps to fill the *cuves* at this *domaine*!

Far left. *No longer in active service, this hefty press stands in the entrance to the Domaine Zind-Humbrecht.*
Left. *Shrouded in mist, Alsatian mountains are breath-taking – as this view from the convent of Sainte Odile demonstrates.*

Léonard Humbrecht, master *vigneron*, insists that the less the grapes are touched and disturbed, the better the wine will be. Who can argue when the Domaine produces no less than four Grand Crus?

Picking is done totally by hand to ensure only the best grapes are selected. And the vineyards are situated in different parts of the countryside to offer the greatest scope for a range of *cépages*. A workforce of nearly 50 people is employed during the *vendange* season, and a yield for the Grand Cru *cépages* of about 30-35 hectolitres per hectare is gained. After the fermentation, the wine is kept in wood right up to the time it is bottled.

Domaine Zind-Humbrecht (*Léonard Humbrecht*)
34 Rue Joffre
Wintzenheim
68000 Colmar
Telephone: 89 27 02 05

DOMAINE LUCIEN ALBRECHT

O R S C H W I H R

The pleasant terraced village of Orschwihr nestles peacefully below the Vosges, whose lower slopes are covered in vines. Here, the tradition of wine-making in the Albrecht family goes back a long way – according to the date engraved on a doorway in their *cave*, to at least 1772.

From the moment you enter the property, on the east side of the village, there are reminders of days gone by. In the far corner of the courtyard, by the entrance to the cave, stands a large 18th century wooden press. And inside there is a fascinating collection of wine-making items. These include an old wooden cask dated 1827 and several curious looking pumps – one from the 18th century and another that resembles an ancient spinning machine.

But the manufacturing arrangements are very much up-to-date, with an impressive display of stainless steel *cuves* of varying sizes. These are vital in the production of a full range of white wine that comes from the 25 hectares of vines around the village. These include the grapes for the Pfingstberg Grand Cru and those for the Bollenberg.

This is a family business, currently under the control of father Lucien and his son Jean, from whom you will receive a warm and enthusiastic welcome. Employed through the year on the property are 14 willing pairs of hands, for there is plenty to do in looking after some of the most southerly of the Alsatian vineyards.

Jean Albrecht holds some very ripe grapes. These have begun to develop the noble rot (pourriture noble) which improves the quality of the juice.

During the summer the Albrechts open their *Maison du Vin* close by in the village. This is an impressive building that dates back from the 17th century, typical of much of the fine Renaissance architecture in Orschwihr.

Domaine Lucien Albrecht (*Lucien Albrecht*)
9 Grand-rue
Orschwihr
68500 Guebwiller
Telephone: 89 76 95 18

CULTIVATING THE VINE

Visit one of the great vineyards of the Médoc region in winter and you could be forgiven for wondering whether it was capable of producing *any* crop, let alone some of the greatest wine grapes in the world. In many cases the vineyard's surface is a mass of pebbles sitting on gravelly soil. The soil is virtually useless for cultivating any other plant except the grape. And for many months of the year the vines themselves are mere blackened stumps of wood. What is responsible for this apparent paradox?

Quality grapes can only be produced under certain climatic conditions. Too far north there will be insufficient sun to ripen them. Too far south and the absence of a winter, during which the vines can lie dormant gathering their strength for the following summer's growth, will produce grapes lacking in flavour and substance.

Fine wine grapes require an average annual temperature of around 15°C; a cool winter; a warm sunny summer with around six hours of sun a day in the growing season (between May and September in the northern hemisphere); and sufficient rain to ensure the grapes produce enough juice. France, apart from the most northern parts, has the ideal climate, although no two years will be exactly the same. This unpredictability means that the wine grown in one place may produce a poor vintage one year and an exceptional one the next.

Certain changes in climate have relatively predictable effects. Generally, the earlier the flowers form on the wine, the better the vintage tends to be. A late frost after the vines have budded (normally in April), or hail while the grapes are on the vine can be disastrous.

Other contributory factors tend to be more subtle in their effect. Two vineyards in the same area, using the identical grape variety and cultivation methods, can still produce quite different wine. These differences are the result of minor variations in climate – each tiny strip of land has what is called its own *micro-climate*.

GROWING FACTORS

The soil is very important too. Great wine can be produced from grapes grown on poor soil (providing it is well-drained), as the vines will be deep-rooted and slow growing. In order to find the nutrients they need, the vines absorb a far wider range and higher concentration of the flavour producing trace elements. There are certain classic combinations of wine and soil types – chalk in Champagne, gravel in the Médoc and large flat stones in the south Rhône – which contribute to the distinct character of the wines from those regions.

The vines tend to be grown from cuttings, rather than pips, to ensure they retain consistent characteristics. By three years old a vine is capable of growing a rather immature grape that will produce a relatively unsubtle wine. The quality of grape and wine steadily improves until they reach an optimum quality/quantity balance at

JANUARY–FEBRUARY

Pruning usually starts in December, but continues for most of the year. Pruning the vines limits their crops – improving the quality of the grapes and thus the wine. Cuttings are taken for grafting on to disease and pest resistant rootstock, from which new vines will be grown.

MARCH–APRIL

Pruning is (temporarily) completed. In mid March the sap begins to rise and the buds appear. The bases of the vines are uncovered. the soil is turned over to aerate it and kill any weeds. The vineyard is tidied up. Last-year's cuttings are taken from the nursery and planted out.

MAY–JUNE

The vines are at their most vulnerable to frost danger in May. The soil is turned over again to kill any weeds. Suckers are removed and the vines are sprayed. The buds flower at the beginning of June. Shoots are thinned out and tied to the wires.

around 15 years of age. After that time the quality will still be high, but yield declines. Most vines are grubbed up and replaced after about 30 years.

Each year after the *vendange* (harvest), which takes place in late September or October, the leafy shoots are trimmed and the soil aerated. In some cases the soil is banked up against the vines as a protection from frost. In steeply sloping vineyards, such as those in the northern Rhône, aerated earth is painstakingly carried back up the slope.

Vine pruning and training may start before Christmas, but is over before the sap begins to rise in March. If the vines are not pruned they expend too much energy producing new shoots, and not enough on grape production. Pruning and training is best done to suit local conditions. In March and April any banked soil is removed and new cuttings, which have spent their first year in a nursery, are planted out.

HAZARDS
TO THE VINES

May is the month during which a sharp eye is kept for frost – using burners to provide heat or sprays to give the vines protective layers of ice. Around the same time, the vines receive the first of as many as 20 sprayings against the many ravaging pests and diseases. The worst of these pests is *phylloxera vastatrix*, a tiny insect which lives on the roots of the vine.

During the 1870s this pest came close to destroying the entire vineyards of Europe, until it was discovered that the roots of the native American vine, from where *phylloxera* originates, was immune to its ravages. Virtually every vine had to be pulled up and replaced by a cutting grafted on to American root stock.

The vine's all important flowering takes place in June. Warm weather and little wind is needed to encourage the bees in their essential pollination duties. By July tiny grapes are visible and the vines can be given a second, limited, summer pruning.

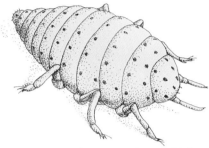

Phylloxera vastatrix, the tiny insect which destroys vine roots, is in fact only about a third of a millimetre long.

In August the grapes ripen, which means that their acidity decreases and their sugar content increases. Later on in the month, spraying against rot, mildew and pests is halted to prevent chemicals being taken up by the grapes.

September is the crucial month – the grapes are at their most vulnerable. Sudden changes in the weather can be disastrous and the grower has to make the ultimate decision – when to pick? That decision is vital and will reflect in the final product – the wine.

JULY – AUGUST

SEPTEMBER – OCTOBER

NOVEMBER – DECEMBER

Vines are sprayed regularly and long shoots are trimmed. Tiny grapes are visible on the vines. Weeding becomes almost as continual a process as pruning. Everything needed for the harvest is prepared. The grapes continue to grow larger and riper.

Spraying and trimming continue until the vigneron decides that the grapes are ripe enough to harvest. The grape's sugar content, the weather throughout the year and the vigneron's wisdom all go to decide the optimum days at which to pick. When the harvest is over the vineyard is fertilized.

Long shoots are pruned and burnt. Soil is ploughed over the bases of the vines to protect them from frost. Any soil that has been washed down slopes must be taken back to the top. Pruning usually begins again before Christmas.

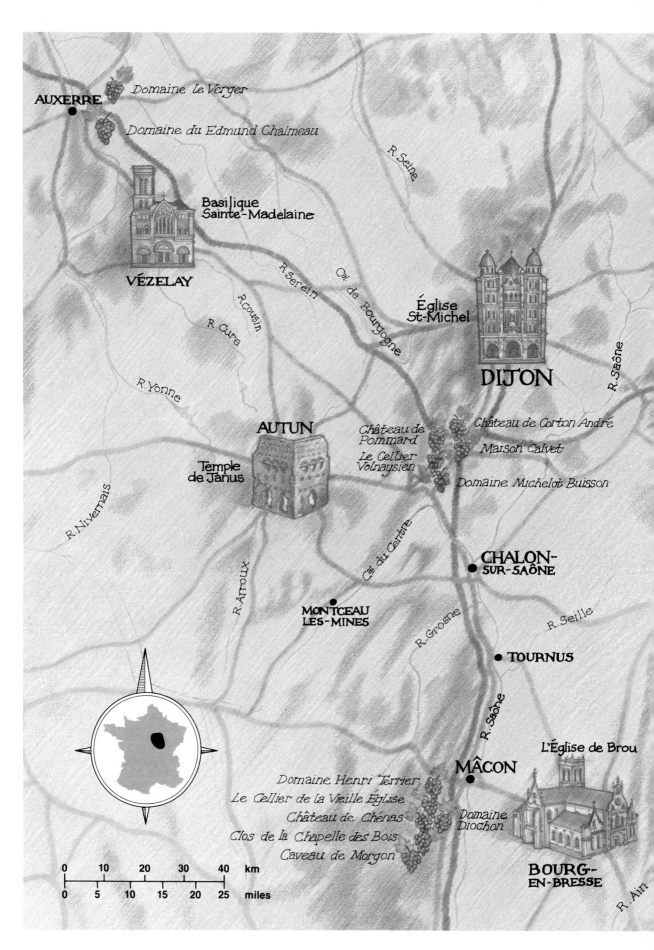

Domaine le Verger

AUXERRE

Domaine du Edmund Chalmeau

R. Seine

Basilique
Sainte-Madelaine

R. Serein

Ca. de Bourgogne

Église
St-Michel

VÉZELAY

R.Cousin

R.Cure

R.Saône

R.Yonne

DIJON

AUTUN

Château de
Pommard

Château de Corton André

Temple
de Janus

Le Cellier
Volnaysien

Maison Calvet

Domaine Michelot-Buisson

R.Nivernais

Ca. du Centre

CHALON-
SUR-SAÔNE

R.Arroux

MONTCEAU
LES-MINES

R.Grosne

R.Seille

TOURNUS

R.Saône

L'Église de Brou

Domaine Henri Terrier
Le Cellier de la Vieille Église
Château de Chénas
Clos de la Chapelle des Bois
Caveau de Morgon

MÂCON

Domaine
Diochon

BOURG-
EN-BRESSE

R.Ain

| 0 | 10 | 20 | 30 | 40 | km |
| 0 | 5 | 10 | 15 | 20 | 25 | miles |

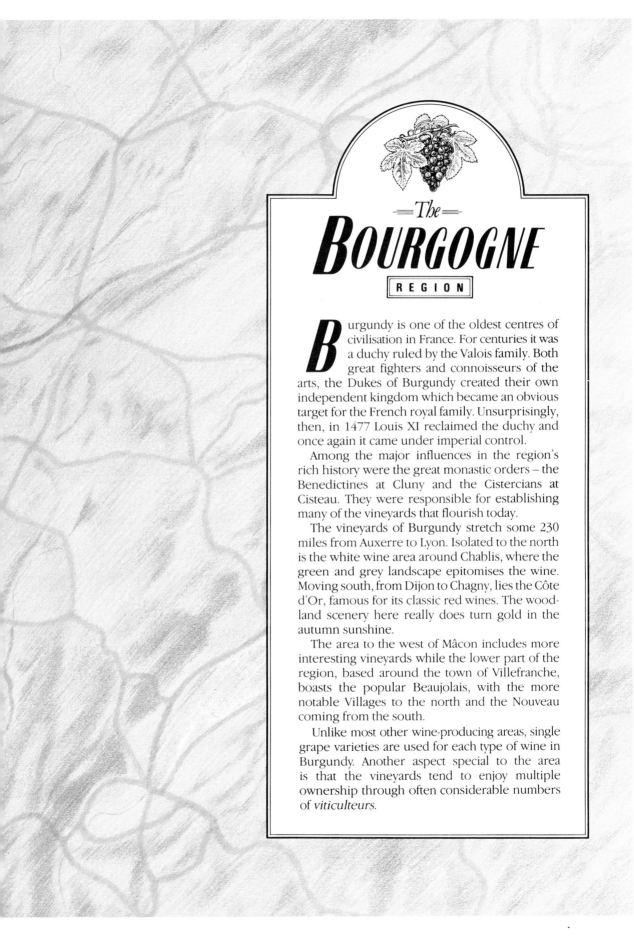

The BOURGOGNE

REGION

Burgundy is one of the oldest centres of civilisation in France. For centuries it was a duchy ruled by the Valois family. Both great fighters and connoisseurs of the arts, the Dukes of Burgundy created their own independent kingdom which became an obvious target for the French royal family. Unsurprisingly, then, in 1477 Louis XI reclaimed the duchy and once again it came under imperial control.

Among the major influences in the region's rich history were the great monastic orders – the Benedictines at Cluny and the Cistercians at Cisteau. They were responsible for establishing many of the vineyards that flourish today.

The vineyards of Burgundy stretch some 230 miles from Auxerre to Lyon. Isolated to the north is the white wine area around Chablis, where the green and grey landscape epitomises the wine. Moving south, from Dijon to Chagny, lies the Côte d'Or, famous for its classic red wines. The woodland scenery here really does turn gold in the autumn sunshine.

The area to the west of Mâcon includes more interesting vineyards while the lower part of the region, based around the town of Villefranche, boasts the popular Beaujolais, with the more notable Villages to the north and the Nouveau coming from the south.

Unlike most other wine-producing areas, single grape varieties are used for each type of wine in Burgundy. Another aspect special to the area is that the vineyards tend to enjoy multiple ownership through often considerable numbers of *viticulteurs*.

The
BOURGOGNE
REGION

*S*tarting a tour of the Bourgogne region from the north, your first call will be to Chablis. *En route*, a stop at the hilltop city of Laon, with its immense cathedral overlooking the Marne, is well worthwhile.

From Laon, Chablis is a comfortable drive and, after paying tribute to the fabulous wines made here, the route to the heart of Burgundy country begins. On the way you should certainly make a stop at the medieval towns of Avallon and Vézelay. The views from Vézelay, in particular, must be among the finest in the whole of France. While in the region, take time to visit the Morvan area, too – a vast spread of forest which is now a national park.

Dijon is the entrance to the Côte d'Or, that golden stretch of vineyards which produce the best, most famous and most expensive burgundies in the world. Dijon is a busy, bustling town with many hotels and restaurants and plenty of opportunities to sample the local specialities – shoulder of lamb grilled over a wood fire, served with a light dressing of the famous Dijon mustard, laced with white wine and herbs, is one delicious example.

The Route des Grand Crus begins at Chenôve, south of Dijon, and runs through the first of the great communes at the lovely village of Fixin, and threads through Gevrey-Chambertin, Morey-Saint-Denis and Vougeot to Nuits-Saint-Georges. Don't miss the famous château at Clos des Vougeot where tastings are held, and be sure to also visit the market at Nuits-Saint-Georges where you'll find a fine array of local produce on sale – from mushrooms to snails.

Moving on to Beaune, the marble quarries at Comblanchien can be seen on the hills. Beaune itself is a must for the traveller. Its attractions include a fine wine museum in the palace of the former Dukes of Burgundy and the famous Hotel Dieu, a medieval hospice, which has a superb Burgundian patterned roof.

An alternative from wine tasting can be enjoyed with a visit to the Spa town of Santenay, beyond Meursault to the south. The thermal waters here were enjoyed by the Romans, and there is also a casino, if you feel the urge to gamble!

Before travelling further south to Beaujolais, take a look at the spectacular rock formations in the valley of Solutre, near Mâcon. This is a strange, exotic area of immense antiquity, where the hills rise in curious shapes like the skeletons of extinct animals. Beaujolais itself is a mountainous area with plenty of places for picnics or simply for feasting on the stupendous views, including the Alps stretching away in the east.

REGIONAL SPECIALITIES

Major types: *Aloxe-Corton, Auxey, Beaujolais-Villages, Beaune, Bourgogne, Bourgogne Aligoté. Chablis, Chambolle-Musigny, Chénas, Clos des Vougeot. Chassagne-Montrachet, Corton, Côte de Beaune-Villages, Fleurie, Gevrey Chambertin, Givry, Juliénas, Meursault,* *Mercurey, Montrachet, Moulin-à-Vent, Musigny, Nuits-Saint-Georges, Pernaud-Vergelesses, Pommard, Pouilly-Fuissé, Puligny-Montrachet, Rully, Richebourg, Romaneé-Conti, Vosne-Romaneé, Volnay.*

The Food
Famous for its rich cuisine, Bourgogne offers plenty of choice and excellent quality. Charolais beef cattle are reared on the region's rich pastures, and the poultry of Bresse is among the best in France – hence a plentitude of coq au vin *and* boeuf bourguignonne. *As well as the* bourguignonne *preparation,* boeuf en meurette, potée, pochouse *and* daube *are delicious dishes. The range of* charcuterie *includes Burgundian ham,* saucisson (sausage) *and* boudin (black pudding) *and among some excellent cheeses are Soumaintrain, Epoisse, Saint Florentin and Morban. And if they are to your taste, snails and frogs legs are readily available, prepared à la bourguignonne.*

Left. An unusual aerial view of a Burgundian domaine.
Below. Harvesting is generally carried out by machine, as you can see here. Very narrow tractors are used to pass between the rows of vines.
Bottom. Traditional hand picking is still favoured by some vignerons who prefer the personal touch.

DOMAINE le VERGER

B E I N E

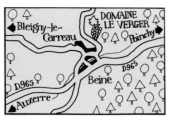

A feature of Chablis is the number of small vineyards, often only a few hectares in area, which provide a livelihood for long-established local families. The Domaine le Verger in the tiny village of Beine is a pleasant example of one of these smaller properties where a modest hand-painted sign, illustrated by a bunch of grapes and the family name, can lead to a fascinating and rewarding experience.

The owner is Alain Geoffroy, whose family has cultivated the precious vines since the time of Alain's great-grandfather.

A spectacular Burgundian scene, as the vineyard workers labour amongst the rows of vines.

Over the years, the property has grown to 25 hectares – planted exclusively with Chardonnay grapes and producing Chablis premier cru.

Alain is assisted by his father Charles, who is actively engaged in the business and welcomes visitors to the cellars, to taste and buy the wines. It is a memorable experience to sit in the cool shadows of the cellars on a hot afternoon and admire the limpid depths of the Chablis – which is as fresh as a spring morning. The wines here are excellent and have won many medals in Paris, Mâcon and Gironde, impressive evidence of their quality.

Domaine le Verger (*Alain Geoffroy*)
4me de l'Equerre
Beine
89800 Chablis
Telephone: 86 42 43 76

DOMAINE du EDMUND CHALMEAU

C H I T R Y

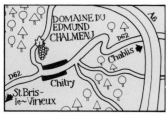

Vines stretch for miles around the village of Chablis, but only some of the wine produced from them can actually be *called* Chablis. This name is jealously guarded and reserved only for the classic French white wine – dry, beautiful in colour and bouquet, but also expensive. However, a lot of excellent wine is made in the surrounding villages from the same grape variety, and in almost identical soil conditions.

The tiny village of Chitry is close to Chablis and produces splendid wines of this type. Chitry marks the beginning of the vineyards of the Yonne Valley, which stretches towards the ancient city of Avallon.

The family of Edmund Chalmeau has been cultivating vines at Chitry for some 200 years. They have an 8 hectare vineyard and running it is very much a family operation. Edmund is helped by his wife, Therese, his three sons and

Left. The village church at Chitry.   *Above*. Thérése Chalmeau and her daughter enjoy a glass of the Domaine's Chablis.

and you should not miss Vézelay, a fortified medieval town perched on a hill, and offering marvellous views of the surrounding countryside. Above the town is the huge church of Saint Magdalen – one of the largest in France at nearly 350 feet long. It has some extraordinary stone carvings and is widely regarded as being a masterpiece of the Romanesque style. It was from Vézelay that Richard Coeur-de-Lion and Philippe-Auguste set out on the third crusade with the English and French armies in 1190.

a daughter. The Chalmeau's are charming people, happy to chat about their wines in the cool cellars. These are made of local stone, and date back at least two centuries.

The area to the south in the Yonne Valley is very attractive,

Domaine du Edmund Chalmeau
20 Rue Ruisseau
89530 Chitry
Telephone: 86 41 42 09

CHATEAU de CORTON-ANDRE

A L O X E - C O R T O N

Not far from Beaune, Aloxe-Corton is one of the loveliest villages of the Côte de Beaune where many of the buildings have the characteristic mosaic rooftops of black and yellow tiles. Château Corton-André, on the slopes of Mont Corton, has a magnificent example of this type of Burgundian roof.

The château is owned by Pierre André – an important firm of growers and *négociants*. The present owner, Gabriel Lioger d'Ardhuy, created an area in the old cellars of the château for visitors wishing to taste and buy the wines of Aloxe-Corton. It's well worth a visit since Château Corton-André produces magnificent red wines and one superb white – Corton-Charlemagne, named after the Emperor Charlemagne who owned the vineyards in 775.

Not far from Aloxe-Corton is the famous Clos-Vougeot, a vineyard of some 50 hectares surrounded by walls (*clos*). This has become something of a French national monument where, by tradition, any passing detachments of the French army stop and salute the vines. With that example, the least the visitor can do is raise a glass in homage.

Château de Corton-André (*Pierre André*)
21920 Aloxe-Corton
Telephone: 80 26 44 25

Many Burgundian rooftops are tiled in this distinctively colourful Flemish style. These are in Beaune.

MAISON CALVET

B E A U N E

Burgundy's wine capital is Beaune, a handsome prosperous town where the leading merchants, or *negociants*, conduct flourishing businesses. Many of them organise tours in the network of cellars beneath the town where the wine is stored.

The famous firm of Maison Calvet is housed in a medieval tower, here in Beaune. It was built in 1477 by the king of France, who had achieved a long-held ambition by taking Burgundy from its duke and adding it to the royal possessions. The fort, with its 10-metre thick walls, was built for the royal army as a refuge against the rebellious townsfolk and it is easy to imagine the army's sense of security behind these massive walls, as the tower has hardly changed over the centuries. Their happiness would doubtless have been complete if it had contained its present liquid treasures.

The director of Maison Calvet is Gerard Bouchard, a member of one of Beaune's most famous wine families. "The Bouchard family history is the history of Beaune," says Gerard proudly as he shows you around the cellars. Here visitors can see all the activity that makes this business a little different from that of other *négociants*, in that storing, racking and bottling are carried out on the premises.

Maison Calvet
6 Boulevard Perpreuil
21200 Beaune
Telephone: 80 22 06 32

Above. The interior of the famous Hotel-Dieu at Beaune, which was built in 1443 and used until 1948 as a charitable hospital.
Far left. Part of the ancient Maison Calvet.
Left. Almost ripe, these grapes hang absorbing the sun's rays.

CHATEAU de POMMARD

P O M M A R D

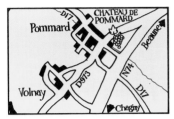

To visit Burgundy without visiting at least one of the region's famous châteaux is unthinkable. The Château de Pommard is one of the grandest, and dates from 1098, although the present buildings were erected at the beginning of the 18th century. The superb 50 hectare vineyard is the largest in the Côte de Beaune. It is owned by Jean-Louis Laplanche who personally supervises the work – and also has the distinction of being a professor of psychology. The vinification is by traditional, time-honoured methods, an important part of which is the use of huge oak casks for storing the wine.

Although the château is visted by thousands of people, it is not over-organised. A sign at the entrance simply asks the visitor to ring the bell and wait for the cellarman. When a few people have assembled, the cellarman appears and takes them on a tour.

The cobbled courtyard of the grand Château de Pommard.

It is reassuring that this duty is not carried out by a professional gude, but by a man who knows and loves the wines of Pommard and speaks of them with devotion.

Château de Pommard (*Jean-Louis Laplanche*)
21630 Pommard
Telephone: 80 22 07 99

LE CELLIER VOLNAYSIEN

V O L N A Y

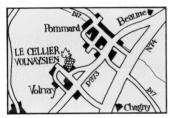

Michel Pont and his family own this charming property in the village of Volnay. As well as the wine cellar there is a restaurant overlooking the sea of vines which stretch away to the horizon. The family also owns vineyards at Château de Savigny, 4 kilometres north of Beaune. The property at Volnay is run by Michel Pont's charming daughter, Nathalie, who is very French and very chic!

The ancient cellar is made of local stone and maintains a constant temperature ideal for the storage of wines. A pleasing thing about a visit here is that there's no obligation to buy. For a few francs you can sip a glass of Volnay (the lightest of all burgundies) and, perhaps, be tempted by the restaurant where regional specialities such as *jambon persille* and *escargots de Bourgogne* can be enjoyed.

Le Cellier Volnaysien (*Michel Pont*)
Volnay
21190 Meursault
Telephone: 80 21 61 04

Far left. The visitor's first view of Le Cellier Volnaysien.
Left. Nathalie Pont – the vigneron's daughter.
Above. The town of Volnay, seen over the surrounding vines.

DOMAINE MICHELOT BUISSON

M E U R S A U L T

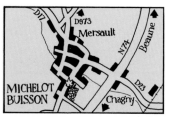

The *domaine* of Bernard Michelot Buisson is far removed from some of the more elegant properties of Beaune, but it is very much a working vineyard. The house is on the edge of the pleasant village of Meursault, and the vines stretch all around it.

Bernard is a typical Burgundian, a jolly, twinkling man who is deeply devoted to his vines. He describes his property as "*typique*" of the Côte d'Or, which it is. But he has a good reputation for producing excellent Meursault, one of the great white burgundies. The main grape variety here is the Chardonnay, but a little Aligoté and Pinot Noir is also grown. It's a family business, of course, in which Bernard is helped by his son, son-in-law and three daughters. Visits to this property must be made by arrangement (a telephone call will do) but it is worth seeing, because it shows the visitor the genuine Burgundy – nothing to do with tourism.

Domaine Michelot Buisson
Rue de la Velle
21190 Meursault
Telephone: 80 21 23 17

DOMAINE HENRI TERRIER

L E S   B R U Y E R E S

Left. *The art of the barrel maker (tonnelier) is alive and well in France. New barrels are used for new vintages as the oak imparts tannin to the wine.*
Above. *Madame Terrier and the rest of the Domaine's reception committee.*

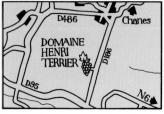

Saint-Amour is a delightful name for a delightful wine and a lovely place to enjoy it is the vineyard of Henri Terrier, just outside the village of les Bruyeres.

Henri and his wife Denise have been at les Bruyères for 20 years producing the wine which has inspired the verse: "*J'aime la vie, J'aime l'amour, Je bois du Saint-Amour*". His son, Robert, helps him with the vines, so you may find you are entertained by Madame Terrier, with the help of her daughter-in-law, Nathalie, and a large, friendly dog called Chiquita.

Although this is a hard-working Beaujolais vineyard, the owners do have time for visitors, inviting them to taste the wines in the cool of the cellars. Here – if you time your visit right – you may be introduced to a taste of the first pressing of the new wine before fermentation. This is a delicious intensely sweet, fruity liquid that has the appropriate name of "Paradis".

Domaine Henri Terrier
Les Bruyères
71570 la Chapelle de Guinchay
Telephone: 85 37 40 05

LE CELLIER de la VIEILLE EGLISE

JULIÉNAS

Juliénas is a sleepy little village, happily settled among swelling, vine-covered hills. This is ancient wine country where the traditional wine-making methods are often followed, and old customs are faithfully observed – such as only bottling the precious wine when the wind is in the north and the moon is on the wane!

Le Cellier de la Vieille Eglise is in the old village church which has become a shrine to wine. Here, the colourful stained-glass windows depict a virile Bacchus surrounded by maidens and sturdy *vignerons*. There is nothing particularly subtle about Beaujolais humour, as these illustrations confirm, but it has an earthy, bucolic charm.

The church is more than a showplace, though, since the wine is actually made here, as you can see during the *vendange* when the members of the *co-opérative*, the *Association de Producteurs du Cru Juliénas*, are hard at work and the village hums with activity. There's a jolly

A quiet spot in the centre of Juliénas.

atmosphere to Juliénas on Sundays when it is traditional for the locals to indulge in a little *dégustation* in an atmosphere of rustic good humour.

Le Cellier de la Vieille Eglise
69840 Juliénas

CAVE du CHATEAU de CHENAS

CHENAS

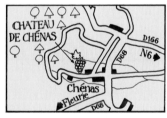

The Château de Chénas has two contrasting rôles – that of an historical building, and the other of a hard-working *cave*. The fine château stands on vine-covered slopes, not far from Moulin-à-Vent. Quite apart from the wine, the property is well worth visiting to enjoy the views of the plain of Saône. Rebuilt in the time of the Sun King, the château is especially impressive if you are lucky enough to visit it during the autumn, when as well as the *vendange* there's a glorious carpet of cyclamen, spreading out under the tall trees that surround the building.

The name Chénas comes from the forest of oak trees (*chenes*) which once covered the hills here. However, they have long since gone, giving way to vines. The *cave* is run by a *co-opérative* of more than 250 growers from Chénas, Chapelle-de-Guinchay, Romanéche-Thorins and surrounding villages. The wine is stored in the château's vast cellars where the temperature never varies, providing an ideal environment for the wine which is kept in oak.

Cave du Château de Chénas
Chénas
69840 Juliénas
Telephone: 74 04 11 91

A ruined windmill, the Moulin-à-Vent, near Chénas is a famous landmark, after which local wines are named.

DOMAINE de DIOCHON

ROMANECHE · THORINS

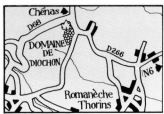

T he name Moulin-à-Vent comes from a sail-less windmill, once used for grinding grain, which commands a breathtaking view of the spreading vineyards of the Haut-Beaujolais.

Bernard Diochon's vineyard is an excellent place to gain a more intimate acquaintance with the Moulin-à-Vent wines, and is virtually in the shadow of the famous windmill. It is typical of many of the small friendly properties common in this region. Domaine de Diochon occupies 4 hectares and produces wine of very considerable quality using traditional methods.

Bernard Diochon is a strapping fellow, splendidly moustached, very outgoing and friendly in the Beaujolais way. The property has been in the family since 1937, and his father, Eugene, although retired, still takes a keen

Vines cluster on the hillsides surrounding one of the many Beaujolais villages. This area is a favourite with tourists.

interest in the vines and makes visitors to the *cave* very much at home. Bernard's wife Josette and their two children, Eric and Stephanie with *grandmére* Marie, make up the rest of the family. These charming people are well worth calling on – for a warm welcome and fine wine, and for the chance to see the true heart of the real Beaujolais.

Moulin-à-Vent is said by some experts to resemble the wines of the Côte de Beaune, especially in good years. Bernard explains that the quality of his wines stems firstly from the age of the vines, which are about 45 years old, and secondly from the character of the soil.

Domaine de Diochon (*Bernard Diochon*)
Romanèche-Thorins
71570 la Chapelle-de-Guinchay
Telephone: 85 35 52 42

CLOS de la CHAPELLE des BOIS

F L E U R I E

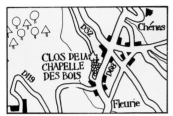

The village of Fleurie is easily found on the Route du Beaujolais – the road which links the wine villages of the region, albeit in a somewhat rambling fashion. Just outside the village is the vineyard of Fernand Verpoix – the delightfully-named Clos de la Chapelle des Bois. It's a handsome property with a substantial house and dark, cool cellars where the wine is stored.

Fernand is more than happy to discuss the mysteries of wine in his cellars, a pleasant occupation on a warm afternoon, and to let you sample one or two wines to illustrate the various points. From the 9 hectares of the property he makes some beautiful wine, very much in the traditional manner, which gains an additional smoothness from being matured in oak.

Typically, the *domaine* is a close family unit. With Fernand are his wife Andrée, son Christian, who is following in father's footsteps, and daughter Natalie, who is still at school.

The vines on this property are mature – some 40 years old – and M. Verpoix thinks they will live to 60 years or more. At this age they will produce less in quantity, but the wine will be of a great quality.

Clos de la Chapelle des Bois (*Fernand Verpoix*)
69820 Fleurie
Telephone: 74 04 10 95

CAVEAU de MORGON

V I L L I E - M O R G O N

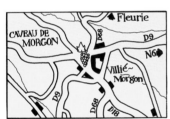

The Caveau de Morgon is ideal for families to visit as there is so much to see. While Mum and Dad investigate the pleasures of Morgon wines in the vast stone cellars under a 17th century château in the centre of the village, the children can explore the gardens which surround the elegant building. These gardens form part of a public park and are beautifully maintained. Peacocks strut across the lawns and there's a small zoo with deer and a large aviary.

This château is no longer the property of a single owner but belongs to local growers and is used as a showcase for their wares. There's a fascinating display of ancient wine tools in the cellars, and the Roman amphorae, discovered locally, shows just how long the vine has been cultivated in this region! There are also some stained glass pictures illustrating the seasons of the vine, and an unusual wooden carving in which a slender leg emerges from a vine-

Above. *Two Morgon vignerons share a tastevin of the caveau's wine. Under this plaque an inscription reads "Le fruit d'un Beaujolais. Le charme d'un Bourgogne".*
Left. *The château – collectively owned by local growers.*

encrusted trunk. Then again it may just be the effect of the powerful Morgon wine!

Many experts have struggled to describe the bouquet of the best Morgon and sophisticated noses have detected such flavours as gooseberries and kirsch. The locals do not struggle in this way – they say "the truth is not in the words: it is in the wine".

Caveau de Morgon
69910 Villié-Morgon
Telephone: 74 04 20 99

VINIFYING THE WINE

Wine is made from grapes by the chemical process known as fermentation. This is caused by the reaction of yeasts on sugar. The result of this reaction is the production of alcohol and carbon dioxide. Any plant that contains sugar can produce wine, but the grape is unique in that the all-important yeast is present naturally on the fruit's skin. In the case of other plants the yeast has to be added.

To start the fermentation process, the yeasts on the grapes' skins have to be brought into contact with the sugar found in the pulp of the fruit. But there's more to this than the mental picture of grape "treading" might suggest. Both traditional and modern techniques of vinification control every aspect of the process in detail.

RED WINE

When the grapes arrive at the *cave* they are crushed and the stalks removed. The resulting pulpy liquid, called "must", is then put in sterilised vats to ferment. Some sulphur dioxide is added to prevent contamination. Fermentation is critically affected by heat, and methods such as water jackets around the vats are used to control the wine's temperature. Red wine is usually fermented at around 25°C. If the grapes are found to lack sugar, it can be added at this stage in order to ensure the correct alcohol content.

The grape skins remain in contact with the must for up to three weeks. This adds colour to the wine and also contributes tannin – the harsh-tasting natural preservative present in grape skins that determines the finished wine's longevity.

In some areas, particularly the Rhône and Midi, a more modern method of fermentation is used, known as *macération carbonique*. Here, whole bunches of grapes are fermented in sealed vats filled with carbon dioxide. The major difference is that no tannin is extracted, and the lack of oxygen concentrates the flavour of the grapes to produce a very fruity wine for early drinking. A similar process is adopted in the Beaujolais region using whole bunches of grapes, but in open containers.

Fermentation continues until either all the sugar has been converted to alcohol or the alcohol level reaches around 15-16% volume, at which the yeast stops working. This rarely occurs naturally and the fermentation will often be artificially stopped to produce a sweeter wine, by adding alcohol or sulphur.

Fermentation can take up to 14 days. When it has stopped the liquid, known as *vin de goutte*, is run off and left to settle. Any remaining liquid is then pressed out of the sediment. This harsh, tannic *vin de pressé* may be added to the wine or, more usually, given to the vineyard workers to drink! The remaining solid mass, the *marc*, is sometimes moistened, fermented and distilled, to produce *eau-de-vie-de-marc*. In other cases it can be used to fertilise the vineyard and return some of the goodness to the land.

After being left to settle, the wine is "racked off" and put in fresh sterilized containers, leaving any sediment

RED AND ROSE WINES

① Red grapes.
② Crusher – crushes stems and grapes together.
③ Juice used to make rosé wine is fermented on the skins for only a couple of days. The skins, the marc, are discarded and usually used for fertilizer.
④ The juice is then run off the skins and fermentation of rosé wine is completed. it has picked up only a small amount of colour and tannin from the skins and stalks.
⑤ Rosé wine.
⑥ Vin de goutte, the free-run red wine is made without pressing the skins and stalks further.
⑦ Remaining liquid is extracted and fermented – vin de pressé, the press wine.
⑧ Red wine

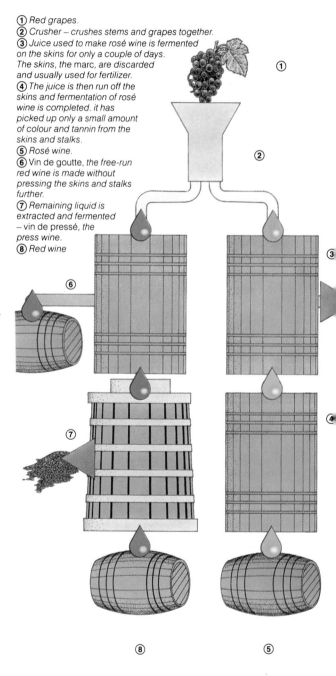

behind. Traditionally these casks are made of wood. The size, shape, age and type of wood affects the final taste of the wine, as does the length of time it spends in the cask. Most wine is left for up to two years in the wood, and from time to time is topped up to replace any that has evaporated.

Before bottling, the wine is filtered or "fined", by adding a substance that will attract the solids that make the wine cloudy and cause them to fall to the bottom of the container. Isinglass (made from the swim bladders of sturgeons), ox-blood and egg white are three traditional fining agents. Blending, *coupage*, of different types of wine is also undertaken at this stage, with the resulting blend being known as a *cuvée*. Some wine is refrigerated to remove tartaric acid.

R O S E   W I N E

The classic way of producing rosé wine is to use red grapes, but to leave the skins in contact with the must for only a day or two. This means that as well as imparting less colour the wine will also contain less tannin. Rosé is therefore best drunk young.

W H I T E   W I N E

The grape skins are removed at the earliest possible stage in the production of white wine. The exception to this rule is if the wine is designed to be kept for a long time – as in the case of the finest white burgundies. Any extra juice is pressed out of the grapes immediately and the solids removed – often with the aid of a centrifuge.

The fermentation of white wine usually takes longer than that of red, and is carried out at a lower temperature – around 15°C. The wide variety of sweetness found in white wines depends not only upon the sugar content of the grapes, but on how long they are allowed to ferment. The *earlier* that fermentation is stopped, the *sweeter* the wine will be. White wine tends to be stored in stainless steel vats rather than wooden casks.

F O R T I F I E D   W I N E

The fermentation of fortified wine is left until only about half the sugar has been converted to alcohol. Then brandy is added to increase the alcohol level and halt the fermentation process. This is why fortified wine is both sweet and strong.

S P A R K L I N G   W I N E

The cheapest – and poorest-quality – sparkling wine is produced by forcing carbon dioxide into still wine in much the same way that fizzy drinks are made. The majority are made by adding sugar and yeast, in a sealed tank, to initiate a second fermentation.

Champagne, and other sparkling wines of quality, is produced under a strictly controlled process – the *méthode champenoise.* In this, the final *cuvée* has sugar and specially developed yeasts added to it. Then it is bottled and kept for about three years.

The bottles are inverted and, over a period, turned so that the yeast sediment settles in the neck of the bottle. Next follows the process called *dégorgement.* The necks are frozen and the bottles opened, so that the sediment is expelled as a frozen lump. Alternatively the yeast is removed with a deft hand operation. Then the bottles are topped up with fresh wine and secured with the special champagne cork and wire cage.

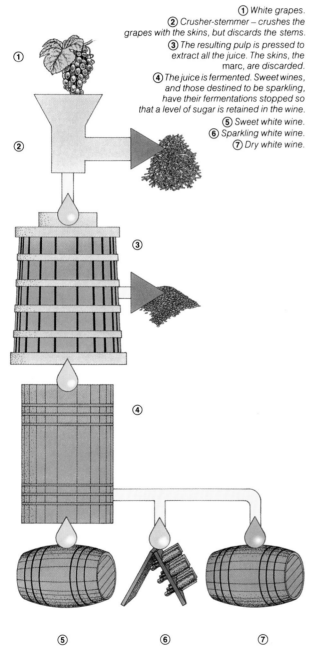

WHITE WINE

① *White grapes.*
② *Crusher-stemmer – crushes the grapes with the skins, but discards the stems.*
③ *The resulting pulp is pressed to extract all the juice. The skins, the marc, are discarded.*
④ *The juice is fermented. Sweet wines, and those destined to be sparkling, have their fermentations stopped so that a level of sugar is retained in the wine.*
⑤ *Sweet white wine.*
⑥ *Sparkling white wine.*
⑦ *Dry white wine.*

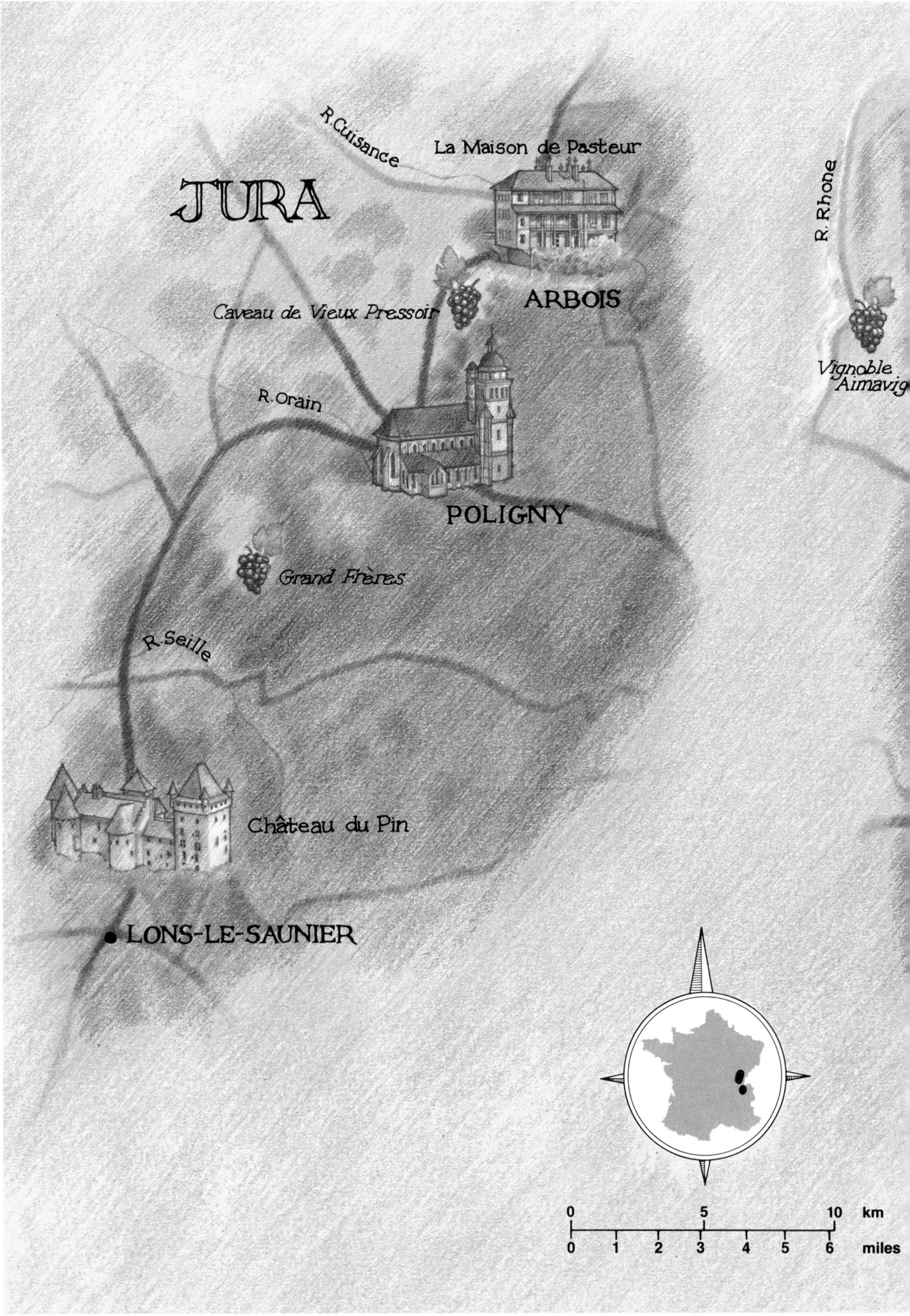

JURA

R. Cuisance

La Maison de Pasteur

R. Rhone

ARBOIS

Caveau de Vieux Pressoir

Vignoble
Aimavig

R. Orain

POLIGNY

Grand Frères

R. Seille

Château du Pin

● LONS-LE-SAUNIER

0					5					10	km
0	1	2	3	4	5	6					miles

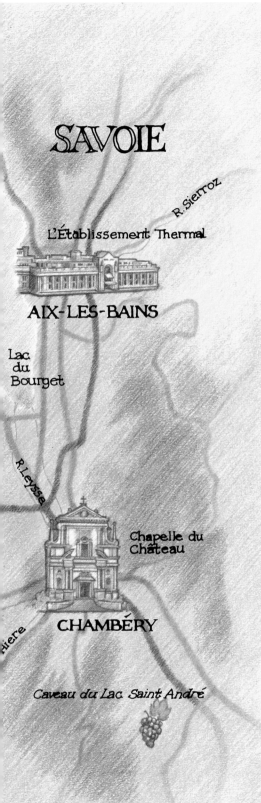

SAVOIE

R. Sierroz

L'Établissement Thermal

AIX-LES-BAINS

Lac
du
Bourget

R. Leysse

Chapelle du
Château

Hière

CHAMBÉRY

Caveau du Lac Saint André

The
SAVOIE & JURA
REGIONS

The Jura and Savoie are two distinct regions to the east of France. Lying to the south-east is Savoie, an area of picturesque and spectacular alpine scenery where time often seems to slip past unnoticed. Although best known for its ski slopes, Savoie's vineyards cover some 2,500 hectares. The tougher grape varieties grown here have adapted to the cold climate to produce some delicious light, mainly white, wine that is as fresh as the mountain air which blows through the vines.

Savoie is a region of contrasts. On the mountain-sides tiny sleepy villages appear to have remained unchanged for centuries, while the popular resort towns on the lakes Léman and Bourget swarm with visitors enjoying the air and scenery. If you're after wine and not skiing, then Savoie is best visited before the winter snows cover the mountains. The pleasing combination of hills, plains and lakes gives much to admire – particularly when tasting the region's good honest wines.

Jura lies to the north-west of Savoie between Bourgogne and the mountains of the Franco-Swiss border. The landscape is natural and unspoiled, and many wild flowers grow freely in the hedgerows.

Jura has a complex history, and the wine trade dates back to Roman times. The vineyards lie at the foot of the Jura plateau, covering just over 1,000 hectares, in an area about 50 miles long and up to 4 miles wide. The wine trade is centred around Arbois, a pretty town with timbered buildings. Here you will find many opportunites to taste the unique local wines. These include a sparkling wine, the specially vinified "straw wine", and the unique *vin jaune* (yellow wine).

The SAVOIE & JURA

REGIONS

The journey from Beaujolais to the Savoie is a magnificent transformation of scenery. Bourg-en-Bresse is probably the best known town in the plain separating Beaujolais and the Swiss mountains. One of the more curious sights here is the famous Bresse chicken, which has become a national symbol with its white body, red wattle and blue legs. Perhaps the best way of obtaining a close examination of these birds is in one of the region's many restaurants – preferably *à la crème*!

Savoie is a region of mountains and lakes. The mountains are vast, rearing dramatically against the skyline. Because the region is remote and farming is on a modest scale, there is little to disturb the flora and fauna, making the area a naturalist's paradise.

Lac de Bourget is France's largest lake, and supports what is almost a navy of pleasure craft. Bourget on the western side is a smart yachting and fishing resort and on the opposite bank is Aix-les-Bains, famous as a spa town.

The gentle, undemanding drive from Savoie to the peaceful Jura is a personal favourite, as driving here is a real pleasure. The roads are virtually deserted and there is a sense of remoteness about the peaceful landscape.

This is rich farming country with mixed arable and livestock agriculture, unlike neighbouring areas which are almost entirely dependent on the vine. The air is pure, exhilarating in the hills, and so clear that the peaks of the Jura mountains can be seen from miles away. The farming is by traditional methods with an absence of chemicals, which results in a profusion of wildlife.

Arbois is the most prominent town, home of the scientist Louis Pasteur, who carried out his experiments on the effect of bacteria on milk, demonstrating that sour milk is not caused spontaneously but is due to microbes introduced through lack of hygiene. This information has of course been of considerable importance to public health and the dairy industry. The wine industry has also been grateful for Pasteur's work, as vinegar is now made only on demand, and does not "randomly" ruin vintages.

Jura is a department of Franche-Comté, a curiously individual region of France. The name actually means "Free Country". Perhaps it is no accident that the philospher Voltaire chose to spend his last days there, in the town of Ferney on the Swiss border.

Like everywhere else in France, there are many delicious things to eat. But there is a special character about the food of the Jura. Try the sliced air-dried beef, bresi, fondues of cheese like those prepared by the Swiss, and a cornmeal mixture which is similar to polenta, the delicacy of the Veneto in Italy.

REGIONAL SPECIALITIES

The Wines
Savoie: *Crépy, Seyssel, Apremont, Vin de Savoie, Roussette de Savoie.*
Jura: *L'Etoile, Château Chalon, Arbois.*

The Food
Savoie: *Cattle raised on the alpine slopes give excellent meat and dairy produce. Cheeses are a major speciality – in addition to the famous gruyère and emmental there are the smoother Beaufort and Roblechon. Naturally many of the local dishes are au gratin, such as gratin dauphinoise (scalloped potatoes) and crayfish. The mountain streams provide excellent trout fishing, and these fish are prominent on the local menus. Look out for biscuit de Savoie á la crème, a delicious spongecake with vanilla custard.*
Jura: *Although not over-rich in specific regional culinary delights, this mountainous area is famous for its wild mushrooms (cèpes, morels and chanterelles), cheeses such as Comté (French gruyère) and Morbier, and Morteau sausages. The range of natural produce also includes trout and mountain-cured ham.*

Left. The church at Myans – a tiny Savoie village near Mon Melian, the scene of a disastrous earth-fall in 1248.
Below. Vines on the hillsides near Château Chalon – a Jura village famed for its vin jaune.
Bottom. A "traditional" farmyard in the Savoie village of Bessans. Bessans is also known for its stone quarries and the village church, which contains some 16th century paintings.

CAVEAU du LAC SAINT ANDRE
S A I N T - A N D R E - L E S - M A R C H E S

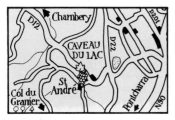

This fascinating property is worth visiting for the journey and the views alone. It is perched on a hillside in a stretch of beautiful country just south of the town of Chambéry, above the lake from which the vineyard takes its name.

Vines cover the slopes surrounding the *cave*, which is owned and run by Jean Claude Perret – an enthusiastic and persuasive advocate of the merits of the wines of the Haut Savoie. He represents the third generation of the family to be entrusted with the care of the vineyard.

There's a small museum at the rear of the cave, with a display of ancient agricultural and wine-growing machinery. This includes an oak wine press dating from 1818, and several venerable machines such as a steam traction engine from 1900 and a Renault tractor of 1928.

It is an ideal place for enjoying a glass of local wine and, perhaps, a snack of local sausages or ham. The view from the cave towards Switzerland is marvellous, and the great bulk of Mont Blanc can be seen on the horizon.

The cave is in a stone cellar, ideal for the *dégustation*, which is followed with enthusiasm by locals as well as visitors. Red, white, rosé and local champagne are available here, but a particularly delicious white wine, Apremont, must take the honours. This is made from a local grape variety, Jacqueres, and is ideal with fish and light meats, but also pleasant on its own as a refreshing drink on a hot day.

Jean Claude is proud of the quality of his wines, many of which have been awarded medals – the Apremont, for example, won gold medals at Annecy and Blayais-Bourgeais in the Gironde in 1986.

Caveau du Lac St André *(Jean Claude Perret)*
Saint-André-les-Marches
73800 Montmélian
Telephone: 79 28 13 32

Right. *View of Saint André and its vineyards.*
Below. *The snow-peaked French Alps give the Savoie a background that is rarely less than breathtaking.*

VIGNOBLE AIMAVIGNE
JONGIEUX

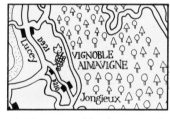

Atiny village, Jongieux is hidden away in the hills of the Haut-Savoie. It has a sense of remoteness and isolation but the local people are delightful, particularly the family Dupasquier who have cared for the vines of Aimavigne for generations.

Noël Dupasquier runs the vineyard with the energetic assistance of his father and mother, both well past retiring age. All work with a vigour that is reflected in the quality of the wines of Jongieux. Noël's wife, Marie Jeanne, offers a charming welcome to visitors who wish to taste the wines in the property's cool and inviting cellar. The couple have three children, so it appears certain the Dupasquiers will continue their stewardship of the vines for some generations to come.

Noël and Marie Jeanne take great pride in their wines, which have won numerous honours. The special character and individual style of the Jongieux wines comes from the grape varieties and from the stone-covered slopes on which they are grown. A range of red, white and rosé wines are made here.

Jongieux does take a little finding, but the effort is fully justified. The easiest way to locate it is to make for the Tunnel de Chat which runs under the Mont du Chat. Take the winding road on the left before the western entrance to the tunnel. From this road, the land stretches out below in a green valley, dotted with lakes which reflect the sun like mirrors. The mountain peaks rise ahead as high as one

Top. The village of Meribel-les-Allues, seen through alpine wild flowers.
Above. The Dupasquier family take a break from their work in the cellar.

climbs. There is breathtaking scenery here, wonderful air, marvellous people and very good wines.

Vignoble Aimavigne (Noël Dupasquier)
Jongieux
73170 Yenne
Telephone: 79 86 82 23

GRAND FRERES
P A S S E N A N S

The lower slopes of the Jura Mountains, rising between France and Switzerland, are covered with vines and there are dozens of little villages where the wine from this distinctive region can be sampled and bought. Grand Frères at Passenans, just off the principal road between Lons le Saunier and Arbois, is a vineyard typical of the area.

It is run by three brothers (hence the name), all of whom are passionately proud of the wines from Jura – their own in particular. The family has its roots deep in the local soil, generation after generation committed to making excellent wine. How long the family has been there is something of a mystery. When asked, the brothers (Lothian, Georges and Dominique) will shrug and say "*toujours*", (always) as if it is the most obvious thing in the world.

There's a large comfortable cellar, ideal for tasting the local wines, especially the most famous of the region – *vin jaune*. This yellow wine has excited the enthusiasm of wine lovers for centuries. The grapes are picked as late as possible, pressed in the usual way and the juice is then put into barrels for between six and ten years. During this time the wine oxidizes and a film forms on the top of the wine. The vin jaune acquires its distinctive colour and nutty flavour during this time and develops even further when in the bottle. The life of the wine is legendary; 50 years is common and locals in the Jura talk of double that time.

When visiting Passenans, you should also go on to Château Chalon, a hilltop village with a view that must be among the finest in the whole of France; a staggering panorama of fields and vineyards stretching away on all sides.

Grand Frères
Passenans
39230 Sellières
Telephone: 84 85 28 88

Right. *Another quiet day in the village of Passenans.*
Below. *A typical countryside scene in the Jura, where vines, pasture and woodland grow side by side.*

CAVEAU du VIEUX PRESSOIR

P U P I L L I N

Above. *Madame Juliet Bulabois, takes in the last rays of an idyllic autumn sun at the Caveau de Vieux Pressoir.*
Left. *The village of Baume-les-Messieurs, named after the monastery founded by Saint Colomba in the 6th century. The existing abbey-church dates back to the 12th century.*

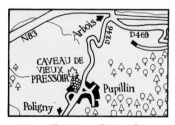

There is a marked contrast between the confident commercialism of Jura's wine capital Arbois and the small, simple villages that surround it. Pupillin, only three kilometres away, is a tiny collection of stone houses, so quiet and undisturbed that dogs sleep peacefully in the middle of the main street during the day. Typical, too, is the property of Georges Bulabois, the Caveau du Vieux Pressoir, where the wines from the surrounding vineyards can be tasted.

The Bulabois family has been here for many generations. George's mother, Juliet, who is well over 70, is a captivating talker about the village and its wines. This is, of course, a family business and every member plays a part, including *grandmère* Juliet – whose duties include producing substantial meals for the men in the fields during the harvest.

A return trip to Arbois can be rewarding and instructive, with a visit to the home of the great scientist Louis Pasteur. Pasteur was born at nearby Dole in 1822, and carried out much of his work when living here. Moreover, the *Office du Tourisme* extends a warm welcome to visitors and has an interesting wine museum at the rear.

Caveau du Vieux Pressoir *(Georges Bulabois)*
Pupillin
39600 Arbois
Telephone: 84 66 02 61

RECOGNISING FRENCH WINES

Facing a huge selection of different wine bottles can be a daunting prospect. How does one begin to make a choice? The most obvious clue to what kind of wine a bottle contains is its shape. Particular regions traditionally use certain bottle shapes.

Even where the wine is produced *outside* France, a bottle shape similar to one of those shown here may be a guide. In California, for example, wines aspiring to reproduce the characteristics of a claret or burgundy use similar bottles to their French counterparts.

Bottle size is important too – the larger the bottle, the longer the wine in it will take to mature. The more usual "bottle" of wine holds 70, 73 or 75 centilitres of wine. Magnums of fine wines, however, sell at a premium. Holding the equivalent of two bottles, they take longer to mature and are felt to achieve the optimum balance between air coming in through the cork and the volume of wine in the bottle.

Half bottle
Uncommon, and relatively uneconomic, way of buying wine. The life of wine in a half bottle is more limited as smaller amounts take less time to mature.

Burgundy bottle
Has sloping shoulders and a punt. Green-yellow glass is used for both red and white wines. Also used for Rhône wines.

Flute
Used in Alsace, this bottle is a tall green version of the standard German flute.

Bordeaux bottle
Used for Cabernet and Merlot wines the world over. Dark green bottles are used for reds and some dry whites. Dry and sweet whites are bottled in clear glass.

Champagne bottle
Always has a punt, and the distinctive lip that retains the cork's wire cage. The glass is thicker than that of other bottles, as it has to withstand the wine's high pressure.

Magnum
The same amount as two bottles of wine – 150 cl. Magnums are preferred for fine wines, as the maturation time is longer – preserving their cellar life.

THE LABEL

The most important feature of the bottle is the label. In France the label of each category of wine must carry certain information by law.

Vins de table must carry the words "Vin de Table de France" or "Vin de Table Français" when sold in France and the words "Produced in France" when exported. The name and address of the bottling company must appear. So must the net volume and, when sold in France, the alcoholic content.

Vins de Pays carry the same information as Vins de Table (with the exception of the alcohol content, which is optional), plus the mention of "Vin de Pays" followed by the place of origin.

VDQS wine labels must name the place of origin and carry the words "Appellation d'Origine Vin Délimité de Qualité Supérieure". They must also display the VDQS guarantee label, name the bottling company and its address, and state the net volume.

All AC wines, with the single exception of Champagne, must say "Appellation d'Origine Contrôlée" on their labels. Alternatively for wine from area X, "Appellation X Contrôlée". The same compulsory and optional information as for VDQS wines also appears. Further details of the classification system are on pages 66-67.

LABEL LANGUAGE

Certain terms are quite widely encountered on French wine labels and give clues to the quality and type of wine to be found in the bottle.

GEOGRAPHY & TYPE

Côtes or Coteaux de X: Usually superior to plain "X" since it is on the *côtes*, the hillsides, that the best vineyards are often sited.

X Villages: Again better than "X" as it comes from one or more special villages in the region of "X".

X supérieur: Not necessarily better than "X", this designates wine of a slightly higher alcohol level.

Primeur: A wine vinified quickly to be drunk young, eg. Beaujolais Nouveau.

BOTTLING

Récolté: Vintage.

Mise (en bouteilles) à la propriété, mise le propriétaire, mise à la domaine: Bottled by the grower at the property.

Mise (en bouteilles) dans nos caves: *Usually* bottled in France in the cellars of the wine merchant named on the label, but can be used by some foreign bottlers to describe "*caves*" in their home country.

Mise par le négociant: Bottled by the shipper who selected the wine.

SPARKLING WINE

Champagne: Made in the Champagne region by the *méthode champenoise*.

Mousseux: Sparkling.

Crément: Slightly less sparkling.

Pétillant: Slightly sparkling.

Perlant: Just fizzing.

Rosé: Pink champagne made by blending with a little red wine.

Reserved for England: Indicates a dry Champagne.

Récemment dégorgé: Recently disgorged.

CLASSIFICATION

Cru classé: "Classed growth", usually meaning a vineyard that has been classified officially. The most famous classification being in the Médoc.

Grand Cru: Great growth, meaning wine from a top vineyard – usually from Burgundy's Côte d'Or, Chablis or Château d'Yquem in Sauternes.

Premier Cru: First growth. In Bordeaux, this designates the five top ranking châteaux. Second to "Grand Cru" for white Bordeaux and Burgundy. Followed by Deuxième, Troisième, Quatrième and Cinquième Crus for Médoc claret.

Cru bourgeois: Médoc claret just under fifth growth level with "Cru Grand Bourgeois" the better of them.

AGE & BLENDING

Vintage: Wine made in one particular year.

Non-vintage: Wine blended from that of several years.

Cuvée: Blend.

Blanc de blancs: Made from white grapes' juice only.

Grand vin: Wine with over 11% alcoholic content.

SWEETNESS

Brut: Very dry.

Extra sec: Dry.

Sec: Slightly sweet.

Demi-sec, Moilleux: Medium sweet.

Doux or Riche: Sweet.

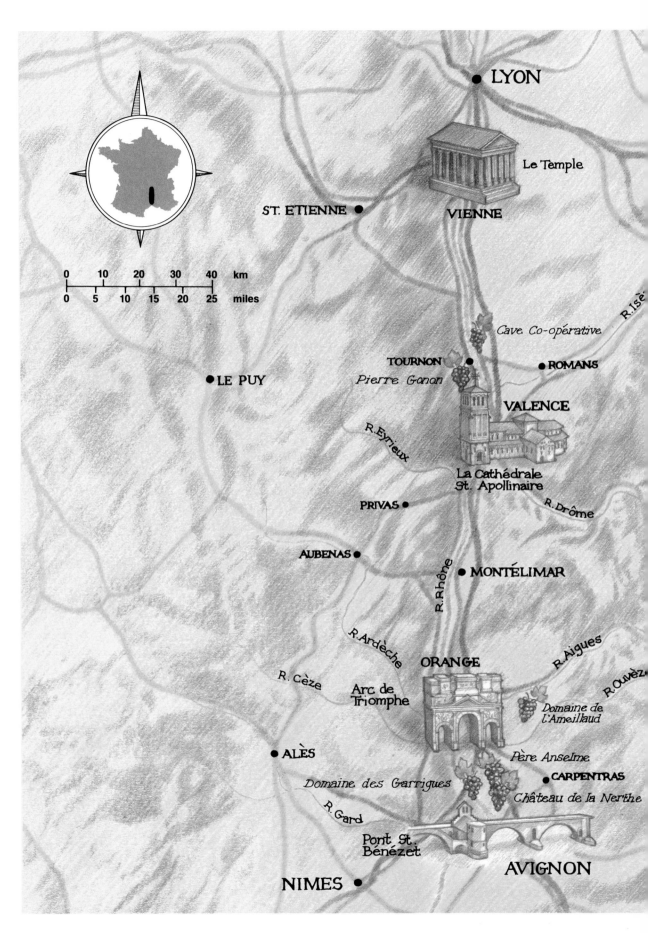

LYON

Le Temple

ST. ETIENNE

VIENNE

R.Isè

Cave Co-opérative

TOURNON

ROMANS

Pierre Gonon

LE PUY

VALENCE

R.Eyrieux

La Cathédrale
St. Apollinaire

PRIVAS

R.Drôme

AUBENAS

R.Rhône

MONTÉLIMAR

R.Ardèche

R.Aigues

ORANGE

R.Ouvèz

R.Cèze

Arc de
Triomphe

Domaine de
l'Ameillaud

Père Anselme

ALÈS

CARPENTRAS

Domaine des Garrigues

Château de la Nerthe

R.Gard

Pont St.
Bénézet

AVIGNON

NIMES

CHAMBÉRY

GRENOBLE

GAP

The COTES du RHONE

REGION

All around the Côtes du Rhône, vineyards dominate the landscape – from the banks of the river Rhône to the rising hills either side. As you travel south the scenery alters quite dramatically – from the oak forests of the northern areas to the scrubland, pines and olive groves of Provence, with its typical Mediterranean flavour. We know the wines produced from the vineyards either side of the river as "Côtes du Rhône". The giant of them all is, without doubt, Châteauneuf-du-Pape, but there are 162 villages which have the right to use the appellation seal of quality too.

The region is steeped in history that can be traced back to the Roman occupation of the 3rd century BC. Vivid indications of this past can still be admired, such as the ancient theatre at Orange and the magnificent aquaduct at Pont du Gard, which brought the water of Uzès to Nîmes.

A wealth of interesting places lies here, just waiting to be discovered. There's Tain, where the first suspension bridge in the world was erected in 1824, the ancient city of Valence – gateway to the Midi, Montélimar, Pont-Saint-Esprit, Beaumes de Venise and many more. And the ruined castles scattered along the rocky peaks overlooking the Rhône provide memorials to the sacrifices made during the Middle Ages.

The COTES du RHONE

The vineyards of Côtes du Rhône follow the mighty river south from Lyon to the former papal city of Avignon. Taking the road to Vienne – "the beautiful" – from the ancient capital of Lyon, you cross over to the right bank of the river and through the terraced vineyards of Côte-Rôtie, Condrieu and Château Grillet. The wines from this area received praise even back in Roman times, from no less distinguished figures than Plutarch and Pliny.

Vienne has much to savour and enjoy, such as the fine Roman theatre, the cathedral and its magnificent churches. Moving on to Valence, your route will then take in a picturesque valley where you can catch a glimpse of the mountains of the Cévennes to the west. And to the north, just before reaching Valence, you'll have the chance to see some of the finest vines in the Rhône, under the appellations of Hermitage, Crozes-Hermitage and Saint-Joseph. Here grapes are grown on the steep hillsides on both banks of the river – around Tain and Tournon – where the views across the Rhône are spectacular, particularly from above Tain l'Hermitage and Mauves. On a fine day you can see the Alps.

Before you enter the historic city of Valence, you'll find two small vineyards nestling below the feudal castle of Crussol – Cornas, whose Syrah grapes produce a fine ruby coloured wine, and Saint-Peray, now known for its fresh sparkling white wine. From Valence the river carries you on towards Orange, through Montélimar – famous, of course, for its nougat. En route to Orange, to the east of the main road, is the village of Suze-la-Rousse. Built on rock and towering over the village is the impressive Château de Suze – which now houses the Université du Vin. Here, the science and culture of wine-making is the focal point of academic study and research.

On through the hillsides, you pass the vineyards of the Rhône Villages and move south to the "dentelles de Montmirail" and the strong, majestic wine of Gigondas.

Orange has many souvenirs of Roman times, with its well preserved Theatre and Triumphal Arch still standing as impressive monuments. To the south, overlooking the Rhône on the left bank, stands the hillside village of Châteauneuf-du-Pape and the most famous of all the Rhône vineyards. The ruins of this important landmark have a grandeur of their own, standing guard over the precious vines that spread around them.

Across the river towards Nîmes are the appellations of Lirac and Tavel, the only part of the Rhône that produces the full range of wines. Here the vines grow on the open plains west of the former papal city of Avignon. The city is renowned for the splendour of its cathedral and Popes' Palace – and, of course, the bridge, which we must all at some time have sung about.

Many Lirac vineyards are spread over ground reclaimed from woods and scrub, a great achievement that has provided some delightful fresh red, white and rosé wine. As well as its wines, Tavel boasts an ancient architectural wonder, the Pont du Gard, still remarkably intact after 2,000 years.

REGIONAL SPECIALITIES

The Wines
Major types: Côte-Rôtie, Château-Grillet, Condrieu, Cornas, Saint-Pernay, Hermitage, Crozes-Hermitage, Saint-Joseph, Tavel, Lirac, Gigondas, Châteauneuf-du-Pape.

The Food
Delicious food accompanies the fine wine from this area, with a definite Burgundian influence to the north and a Mediterranean flavour to the south. Mouth-watering dishes include pintadeau (young guinea fowl) aux olives sur canapés, quenelles de brochets Nantua (pike) and matelote d'anguilles (eels in red wine). Among other interesting local dishes is salade de pissenlits aux lardons (dandelion and bacon salad), and what better way can there be to end a meal in the region, than with a slice of tarte Lyonnaise (a custard tart with Kirsch and almonds). In fact Lyon boasts some of the area's best cuisine, with specialities such as tablier de sapeur and petit salé. Among the goat cheeses, from the Mont d'Or, try rigotte de Condrieu or cervalle de Canut which is made with herbs.

Top. Dramatic cliffs tower over the river Ardéche, near the village of Balazuc in the Rhône valley.
Above. The ornate 14th century astrological clock at Lyon's cathedral of Saint Jean.
Left. The Pope's Palace (Palais des Papes) in Avignon. Building was started by Pope Benedict XII, who was elected in 1334.

CAVE CO-OPERATIVE

T A I N   L ' H E R M I T A G E

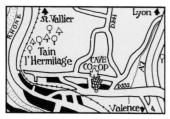

The Cave Co-opérative at Tain L'Hermitage is situated below the vine-covered hillsides bordering the east bank of the Rhône, which dominates the picturesque valley through which it majestically flows. Some 500 growers bring their harvest down from the hills to be made into one of the five appellation wines from this part of the Côtes de Rhône region. They have been doing so for more than 50 years, and in that time have seen the fruits of their labour grow with the success of this large, well-organised winery.

Founded in 1933, the *co-opérative* then produced some 4,000 hectolitres of wine. Today, under the direction of Michel Courtial, more than 40,000 hectolitres are handled each year. You could say it's something of a family business, since M. Courtial's father was the first director here.

Naturally, traditional methods of vinification have been maintained at Tain L'Hermitage, although the *cuvaison* lasts up to two weeks – a little longer than for some other red wines. One item M. Courtial is proud to show is a bottle of 1933 vintage – the only one left. However, many other early vintages are kept in the bottle stores, deep in the heart of the *cave*.

Although red wine does account for the vast majority of the production, about 20% is given over to producing some quite excellent white wine; such as the 1982 Hermitage Blanc.

The laboratory at the co-opérative *is used to analyse and assess the quality of the members' wine.*

When you have had a look round the *co-opérative* and sampled a selection of the excellent wines in the large but pleasant *dégustation* area, you should take a trip to the viewpoint on the hill above Tain L'Hermitage. It is quite breathtaking. On second thoughts, perhaps you should do this first!

Cave Co-opérative de Vins Fins de Tain L'Hermitage
22 Route de Larnage
BP No 3, 26600 Tain-L'Hermitage
Telephone: 75 08 20 87

PIERRE GONON, VIGNERON

M A U V E S

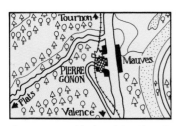

When you visit the home of Pierre Gonon, be prepared for plenty of pleasant surprises. The Gonon family live in a modest house near the edge of the village of Mauves – just off the main road behind the church. When you meet M. Gonon here you will hopefully be offered a short trip round his vineyards. Don't refuse, but make sure you leave your car behind.

For M. Gonon's vines grow over approximately 3 hectares on the steep hillside above Mauves, across the railway line. They are accessible only along rough, well-rutted tracks, but the view is quite superb and well worth the effort. It is surpassed only by that from the Chemin de Paradis (aptly named), from where you look out across the Rhône Valley.

M. Gonon and his charming wife Jeannette run the vineyard with some help from their younger son, when he's

Pierre Gogon's hillside vines, high above Mauves.

not at school. The highlight of the visit is without doubt the *cave*. Don't be put off when you are led to a set of garage doors opposite the house – behind these lies a winery full

Far left. *The Pont d'Arc, a natural bridge that crosses the Ardéche.* **Left**. *Pierre Gogon takes a glass of wine from a barrel in his winery.*

of delights. There is, for example, the huge vat where the Gonons still tread the grapes, and a wooden *cuve* that's centuries old – but no longer used!

You then descend into the lower part of the *cave* for the *dégustation*, deep underground, where M. Gonon keeps his precious Saint Joseph wine. Your glass will be filled by pipette, and you should linger here to savour not only the richness of the wine but also the atmosphere.

You would think Pierre Gonon had more than enough to do keeping his business going. But he also grows cherries and apricots, and still finds time to perform his duties as president of the Saint Joseph Appellation. Moreover, this delightfully natural, unassuming man will always find time to give you an irresistible welcome.

Pierre Gonon
Rue des Launays
07300 Mauves
Telephone: 75 08 07 95

DOMAINE de l'AMEILLAUD
C A I R A N N E

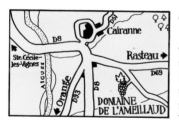

The Domaine de l'Ameillaud, with its 56 hectares of vines, lies to the east of Cairanne. This is one of four villages in the area to benefit from the right of Appellation Villages Contrôlée.

In fact, the Domaine de l'Ameillaud is one of three properties grouped together in 1967, the others being Domaine le Château and Domaine la Beraude. Le Château dates back to 1790 when its owner, the mayor of Cairanne M. Bagnol, began wine production. It has remained in the family ever since.

The production from the three properties is essentially of red wine, with l'Ameillaud providing the centre for wine-making and storage. When I visited there was capacity for 8,000 hectolitres, 1,000 of which were kept in oak casks, but plans were being made for an expansion.

Interestingly, this is one of very few vineyards in the Côtes du Rhône that is run by an Englishman – Nicholas Thompson, who married Sabine Rieu, a descendant of the Bagnol family. They offer a warm welcome to visitors in a remark-

ably French style. You can visit the winery and see the large oak casks that contain the best of the red wine. There are two old-fashioned presses which are kept in working order – just in case. And you will then be invited into the house to taste some of the wines that have made these vineyards such an important part of the area's wine production.

Domaine de l'Ameillaud *(Nicholas Thompson)*
84290 Cairanne
Telephone: 90 30 82 02

The Domaine de l'Ameillaud seen over the harvested vines.

CHATEAU de la NERTHE

C H A T E A U N E U F - D U - P A P E

A pilgrimage to the home of the most famous of all Rhône wines, Châteauneuf-du-Pape, should certainly include a visit to Château de la Nerthe. This stands majestically among trees on rising ground just to the east of the hilltop town.

At the time of my visit, the château was undergoing extensive renovation and repair. It has an impressive history that goes back to the 16th century, making its vintages among the oldest of Châteauneuf. In 1599 the first vines were planted here by the De Villefranche family; by the 18th century the château's reputation for wine had spread throughout Europe and even as far as the United States.

In more recent years the château, under private owner-ship, fell into neglect. However, in 1985 its new owners, David et Foillard, began the mammoth task of restoring the property and its vineyards to their former glory. What I saw at the time of my visit was a remarkable transformation in such a short space of time. Much work still had to be done on the château and the vines, but the facilities being created for the production of wine will surely assure La Nerthe of a lasting recovery to something of its former glory.

There is a quite startling blend of tradition and technology at La Nerthe. To come from the almost clinical stainless steel *cuves*, regulated by computer to ensure exactly the right fermentation temperature, into the well restored cellars, where the wine is left to age, is like bridging centuries of history in one step.

When you have completed your visit around the grand, highly atmospheric network of underground cellars, you can enjoy a little taste of some quite delicious red wine in the intimate *caveau* set aside for the *dégustation*. All this is a rare treat you should certainly not forget.

Château de la Nerthe
Route de Sorgues
84230 Châteauneuf-du-Pape
Telephone: 90 83 70 11

Far right. Stony ground typical of the area around Châteauneuf du Pape. Heat absorbed by the stones is released at night, protecting the vine roots from frost.
Right. Château de la Nerthe.

PERE ANSELME

C H A T E A U N E U F - D U - P A P E

MUSEE du VIN

No visit to the Côtes du Rhône region would be complete with-out stopping at the old town of Châteauneuf-du-Pape; built on top of a hill and made world famous by its wines. While you're there, you are strongly recommended to call at Père Anselme's, where the history of wine-making in all its aspects is admirably laid out in a fascinating museum.

There is so much to look at and enjoy here, but out-standing exhibits include a wooden cask from the Middle Ages, which held 4,000 litres of wine, and a 16th century press. You can also taste a whole range of wines from the Rhône Valley.

Thanks for this enlightening collection must go to Jean-Pierre and Jacqueline Brotte. Their imagination and endeavours have carefully and successfully recreated a history of wine and its culture that has few equals.

Père Anselme (Jean-Pierre Brotte)
BP No 1, 84230 Châteauneuf-du-Pape
Telephone: 90 83 70 07

DOMAINE des GARRIGUES

R O Q U E M A U R E

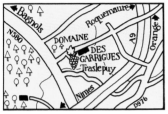

Around the start of the 1960s, much of the land that now makes up some of the best vineyards in Lirac was just woodland and scrub. The transformation came about through the energy and determination of Jean-Claude Assémat who, having bought up about 300 parcels of land, created the Domaine des Garrigues in 1963.

It was a bold venture, but one that has certainly paid off. In the years since the land was cleared, cultivated and the vines established, M. Assémat's wines have won a host of top awards.

The main property stands on open ground just off the main road to Bagnoles, near the village of Roquemaure. This is on the other side of the Rhône from Avignon and the classic wine-growing area of Châteauneuf-du-Pape. Undaunted by his more illustrious neighbours, M. Assémat

above the fascinating fortified church of Saint-Laurent. From this point you have a magnificent view across the Rhône, and over a large part of the region.

At Garrigues, the winery receives the harvest from all the vineyards. The traditional methods of vinification are used here. Among the interesting features are some underground *caves*, which go down nearly 13 metres (40 feet) below the surface. These are used for the red wines.

Visitors are welcome at the *cave*, where a tour of the facilities can be arranged. After that you can taste and enjoy some of the best wines that Lirac can offer.

Domaine des Garrigues (*Jean-Claude Assémat*)
30150 Roquemaure
Telephone: 66 89 23 52

Top right. *Casel Oualou is one of the properties that make up Jean-Claude Assémat's Domaine des Garrigues.*
Above. *The man himself! Jean-Claude Assémat and companion Bruno at home.*
Right. *Hillside vines undergo close scrutiny.*

has confidently developed this once barren land, which now produces the grapes for some excellent AC wines.

It is interesting that this is one of only a few places where the full range of wines – red, rosé and white – are made. The vines now cover some 60 hectares and the estate includes the Domaine des Causses et Saint Eynes, crossing the communes of Saint-Laurent-des-Arbres and Saint-Victor-la-Coste.

Here the vineyard spreads across the rising ground

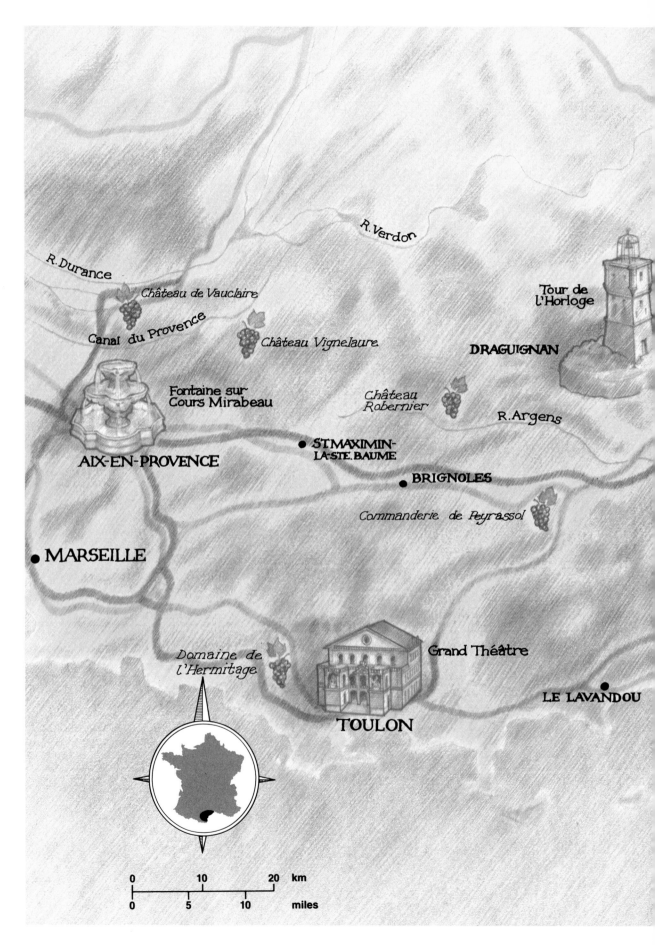

R. Verdon

R. Durance

Château de Vauclaire

Tour de
l'Horloge

Canal du Provence

Château Vignelaure

DRAGUIGNAN

Fontaine sur
Cours Mirabeau

Château
Robernier

R. Argens

St MAXIMIN-
LA-STE. BAUME

AIX-EN-PROVENCE

BRIGNOLES

Commanderie de Peyrassol

MARSEILLE

Domaine de
l'Hermitage

Grand Théâtre

LE LAVANDOU

TOULON

| 0 | 10 | 20 | km |
| 0 | 5 | 10 | miles |

GRASSE

R. Siagne

Théâtre Romain

FRÉJUS

ST. RAPHAËL

Domaine de
la Vernède

STE. MAXIME

ST. TROPEZ

The PROVENCE
REGION

A visit to Provence is an ideal follow-on from a tour of the Côtes du Rhone. On entering the region, just a few kilometres south of Avignon, the brilliant blue sky and warm sun of the midi will reach out to welcome the traveller. But it is further south, around the thriving university town of Aix-en-Provence, that the area's vineyards begin to appear on the craggy hillsides.

Visitors could be forgiven for wondering how this small strip of land lying close to the sea produces such excellent wine every year. The answer lies in the rich soil found in relatively small pockets in three main parts of the region. This, together with the abundance of sun, ensures that the juice-filled grapes will provide the unique flavour of Provence wine.

Provence is among the oldest wine producing areas of France, and records show that the very first vines were planted here by the Greeks way back in 600 AD. But despite its pedigree, the area has a chequered history, and only achieved VDQS status for its premier wines in the early 1950s. Luckily, tourists have helped spread the word about Provence wines, which can now be bought world wide.

The individuality of the vineyards is reflected in the very distinctive taste of each *vigneron's* wine. In many cases the table wines are so localised that they add extra pleasure when accompanying the food of each area, which can range from freshly landed seafood to rabbit and wild boar. And there can be few delights to compare with a local vintage and a speciality dish of the region, enjoyed under the stars on a warm evening in Provence.

The PROVENCE

REGION

No visitor to Provence can resist the temptation to see the beautiful blue Mediterranean lapping at the craggy, rock-strewn coastline – the Côte d'Azur. So an ideal starting point for any tour is at Le Beausset.

This small town is at the centre of the Bandol wine region, only a few kilometres from the sea. Its friendly hotels and restaurants provide a perfect resting place for the visitor to the region and its vineyards. Taking the coast road for a short while from Le Beausset provides an enjoyable start to any day and, turning inland towards Sollies-Pont and Cuers, you'll find a pleasant route leading among flat fields of corn and maize. Taking the smaller country routes at Carnoules you can wend your way to Flassons-sur-Issole and the delights of the Commanderie de Peyrassol.

The tall "umbrella pines" become a feature of the landscape as the visitor heads towards the more hilly part of the Var. On leaving the Commanderie, there are many options for the onward route to Puget-sur-Argens and the Domaine de Vernède. The N7, although a main road, offers a quick solution.

Good accommodation is available at the seaside resorts of Frejus and Saint-Raphaël, or further inland at villages like Bagnols-en-Foret or Fayence. Saint-Raphaël is a grand, rather old-fashioned resort, whose splendours have recently been revived. The casinos mingle with churches in true Côte d'Azur tradition, and overlook the gently rocking fishing boats in the busy harbour.

Inland, the hillside town of Fayence offers spectacular views of the surrounding countryside. The town itself has countless steps leading between the tree-lined squares and terraces that show the visitor an intriguing myriad of Provence architecture.

This route to Montfort-sur-Argens passes along twisting secondary roads through the main inland wine-growing regions. Occasionally, superb views towards the coast can be glimpsed through the pine forests.

The climb towards Barjols begins after the sleepy village of Montfort. Villages which barely seem able to cling to the hillsides each offer their own tranquil charm. The hotels and restaurants to be found in these little towns give the traveller a welcome relief from the blazing sun or blustery Mistral winds, which form a regular feature of the Provençal climate.

The last stretches of the road to Barjols is cut through impressive craggy hills that spill water from clear mountain streams. Umbrella pines and cork oaks dot the roadside and contrast with the austere grey rock of the landscape.

At Barjols there is a stunning waterfall beside the town's square. In fact water makes quite a theme here, as the town has 33 fountains! Moving on to Rians, the ornate church and the Hotel de Ville, along with the centre of the town have been superbly renovated. Outside the town, en route to Château Vignelaure, *sanglier* – wild boar – can be seen on either side of the road.

REGIONAL SPECIALITIES

The Wines
Major types: *Cassis, Bellet, Bandol, Palette, Côtes de Provence, Côteaux d'Aix-en-Provence.*

The Food
Provence is a region of herbs, garlic and the traditional onion and tomato sauce. Seafood is, of course, a must with the famous bouillabaisse (fish stew), red mullet, morue aioli (salted cod with garlic mayonnaise) and thon à la provençale (tuna). There is the local version of the

pizza, pissaladière, soupe au Pistou (with vegetables and basil) and gigot au romain (lamb with rosemary). Stuffed aubergine,

"floating islands" (oeufs à la neige) and tarte Tropézienne are just a few of the many specialities.

Top. Approaching Saint Tropez the glamorous way – by motor
launch from a yacht!
Left. A typically French village shopkeeper and her wares.
Above. Harvesting lavender in the Provençal countryside.

DOMAINE de l'HERMITAGE

LE BEAUSSET

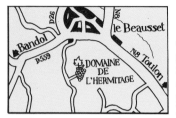

Le Beausset is a small town near the centre of the Bandol wine region. This area stretches for just a few kilometres east and west of the town and down to the Mediterranean. To the south of Le Beausset there is a rather solitary hill, covered in vineyards. It is virtually on the top of this hill that you find the vineyard of Gerard Duffort – the Domaine de l'Hermitage.

M. Duffort is a senior member of the Bandol Vineyard Association and is a fountain of knowledge about the people and wines of this tiny region of Provence. His own vineyard boasts modern facilities which are used to produce Bandol wine of excellent quality. Domaine de l'Hermitage covers an area of 36 hectares and is largely planted with Grenache and Mourvèdre grapes. Vinification is by the natural process, and in most cases the wine is left to mature for at least 18 months before being sold.

Right. Gerard Duffort stands proudly by his vines.
Below. Some of the Domaine de l'Hermitage's 36 hectares of vines.

The *cave* itself, although of relatively late construction, is cool and extensive. The spotless metal vats and clean piping mean that the wine can flow from vat to bottle with little human involvement. The tasting room offers a pleasant atmosphere. Here M. Duffort is happy to spend time relating the finer details of Bandol wine, which he naturally thinks is among the best in France.

Domaine de l'Hermitage (Gerard Duffort)
Le Rouve
83330 Le Beausset
Telephone: 94 98 71 31

COMMANDERIE de PEYRASSOL

FLASSANS

Leaving the hustle and bustle of the main road from Brignoles to Nice, visitors to the Commanderie de Peyrassol suddenly find themselves on a rough, dusty track that leads through pines and vines to the tranquil setting of a large farmhouse. And they will doubtless be struck by the stark contrast between the pressure of modern day life and a vineyard that has changed little since 1256.

Françoise and Yves Rigord, who own and run the 150 hectares of vineyard, are committed both to the wine they

produce and the preservation of the friendly, tranquil atmosphere of the Commanderie. As M. Rigord opens the solid wooden door of his *cave*, you can almost smell the history – hardly surprising, when you consider one part of the *cave* dates back to the 13th century.

It was in this cellar of the Commanderie that the Knights Templar first vinified a grape harvest in 1256. Then in 1311 the Knights of Malta took the estate and ran it until the French Revolution. M. Rigord's family bought the land from the state in 1870 and has continued to run it until the present day.

Grenache, Cinsault and Mourvèdre grapes are used to make Peyrassol's rosé wine, while Syrah and Cabernet Sauvignon provide the vital ingredients for the red. The

vinification method used at the Commanderie is a natural process which involves draining without crushing. This is carried out at low temperatures to encourage the wine to acquire a deeper colour and a fruitier taste.

The *cave* itself also offers a tasting section where visitors who have survived the beaten earth floor and cooler temperatures of the wine store can enjoy the Commanderie's wines. For those who prefer the sun, there is an opportunity to taste the products of the Commanderie overlooking the gardens of the magnificent farmhouse.

Commanderie de Peyrassol
(Yves et Françoise Rigord)
83340 Flassans
Le Luc en Provence
Telephone: 94 69 71 02

DOMAINE de la VERNEDE
P U G E T - S U R - A R G E N S

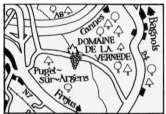

A few kilometres north of the bustling Mediterranean resorts of Frejus and St Raphaël lies the Domaine de la Vernède, a small family-run vineyard, with 24 hectares of vines.

The road to the Domaine is little more than a track which bends between rows of beautiful fruit trees and vines. The journey to the *cave* adds greatly to the atmosphere of the Domaine and at fruit picking time many visitors stop en route to watch or just to inspect the well pruned trees.

The *cave* itself is found in the centre of the vineyard, sheltered from the glare of the sun by tall plane trees. There is nothing grand about the *cave's* exterior, which resembles an ancient stone barn. But once inside the small wooden entrance door, you will find a cavernous area packed with enormous wooden wine vats. The huge stone flagstones and high ceilings add to the cool, calm atmosphere.

The *propriétaire*, Audie Garrassan, recommends that the Domaine's wine, which is either red or rosé, should not be kept near the sea. This is interesting when you consider that the vines themselves can be no further than a few kilometres from the Mediterranean. M. Garrassan allows his wine to ferment for six days before it is put into the huge wooden vats that fill both areas of the large *cave*.

One rather unusual practice here, is the use of mats rather than metal rollers to press the grapes. With due encouragement M. Garrassan will show visitors around the *cave* and chat happily about the problems of producing Domaine de la Vernède wine.

Domaine de la Vernède *(Audie Garrassan)*
83170 Puget-sur-Argens
Telephone: 94 51 22 55

Beautiful countryside is another of Provence's many assets.

CHATEAU ROBERNIER
MONTFORT - SUR - ARGENS

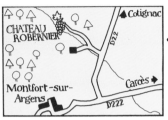

Just 4 kilometres north of Montfort-sur-Argens, where the vines meet the road on either side and distant rocks reflect the harsh Mediterranean sun, you can find Château Robernier. The small rough track that leads towards the Château winds between the vines of an adjacent vineyard and the visitor can be forgiven for stopping to admire the property once it comes into view round the final bend. Unlike many large houses in the Provence region, Château Robernier is a turreted fairy-tale building, which gives it an outstanding appearance from its site on a slight hill. The main parts of the Château date back to the 15th century and the surrounding gardens are a further joy, the vineyard being owned by M. Croisy whose fascination for exotic plants adds to the interest and atmosphere of the place.

Entering the central courtyard of the Château through a stone archway, you find a cool atmosphere in which M. Croisy will happily discuss his wine making methods. Red Côtes de Provence wine is produced at the Château together with white and rosé. It is exported to many countries, but is a particular favourite of the Swiss.

Château Robernier (M. Croisy)
83570 Montfort
Telephone: 94 64 49 11

Right. Unusual in Provence, Château Robernier is a turreted, fairy tale building.
Below. Redundant vats rest in the Château's grounds.

CHATEAU VIGNELAURE
RIANS

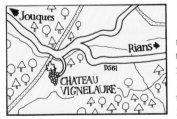

Rians is a delightfully preserved Provençal town that benefits from the existence of a by-pass for main traffic, which leaves it virtually undisturbed. Heading east from the village towards Peyrolles, the traveller passes farms where the wild boar (*sanglier*) is bred to provide targets for hunters at the start

Roses add the perfect finishing touch to these rows of vines at the Château Vignelaure.

of the hunting season in October. Few, if any, vines are in evidence on this route until you reach the fine stone entrance of Château Vignelaure. Here, the neat rows of carefully tended vines are a pleasing sight. The metalled driveway that leads to the Château is also superbly kept and the visitor is left in no doubt that this vineyard is proud of its wines, made from the grapes planted by Georges Brunet back in the sixties.

From the outside, the neat Spanish-style buildings could give visitors the idea that, apart from the fine wine, little of interest is to be found within the walls of Château Vignelaure. This, happily, is a false impression, and one that M. Brunet's guides are quick to dispel. A short walk from the business-like château office brings you to the door of the *cave*. Once inside, the wide and spacious entrance hall with its tiled floor offers a glimpse of things to come. It is decorated with large atmospheric black and white pictures of previous château owners and the local people enjoying the fruits of their labours.

When the guide switches on the lights in a tunnel that leads from the wine store to the wine vaults, the visitor is presented with an Aladdin's cave of wine. This, as the guide explains, contains bottles of every year's production.

More importantly, between each neat stack of bottles, are works of art which grateful customers have donated to the château. It has become an accepted practice for artists who enjoy Château Vignelaure wine to provide an original work of art for the *cave*, or in some cases to paint directly onto the stone walls. The result is a collection of original work which delights the visitor.

Château Vignelaure (*Georges Brunet*)
83560 Rians
Telephone: 94 80 31 93

CHATEAU de VAUCLAIRE

M E Y R A R G U E S

S ettled beside the River Durance, between Peyrolles and Meyrargues, are the plain-looking buildings of the Château de Vauclaire vineyard. Only the large field of sunflowers just inside the entrance offers a spectacular sight. But however plain the exterior, the welcome offered to visitors by the *propriétaire*, François Sallier, is colourful to say the least. Although officially retired, M. Sallier enjoys

both wine and people and is never happier than when he is talking about wine making to interested listeners.

Inside his cave there is a wealth of plaques and certificates which bear witness to the quality of M. Sallier's wine – not least of which is a gold medal from the Paris Wine Fair awarded for his 1983 Coteaux d'Aix red. Although the vats are metal and the *cave* is clean and purpose-built, visitors are left in no doubt that it is M. Sallier's special magic that produces the excellent wine.

The vineyards themselves lie between the Château and the modern canal, which was built by Electricité de France alongside the River Durance. As M. Sallier explained, some vines were lost when the canal was built, but we must presume that the electricity company offered ample compensation.

With a patron willing to while away the time talking about his wine, this vineyard is a pleasure to visit. It is vital, however, that visitors understand French, because with his Provençal accent and love of wine M. Sallier can sometimes be a little difficult to understand.

Château de Vauclaire (*François Sallier*)
13650 Meyrargues
d'Aix-en-Provence
Telephone: 42 57 51 44

Above right. *The cave at Château de Vauclaire – home of some exceptional wine.*
Above. *The* propriétaire, *François Sallier.*

WINE CATEGORIES

All the world's major wine producing countries have a classification system which enables the consumer to judge the relative quality of the product. The European Economic Community (EEC) regulations recognise two main categories of wine: "table wine" and "quality wine produced within a designated region".

The second, higher quality, category has its own additional regulations regarding grape type, cultivation and vinification methods, maximum yield and so on. So the most important thing you need to know is, where was the wine produced?

In France the two broad EEC categories are each sub-divided so that French wine falls into one of four types. In ascending order of quality these are: general vins de table; vins de pays; Vins Delimité de Qualité Supérieure (VDQS) and Appellation d'Origine Contrôlée (AC).

VINS DE TABLE

These can be produced in France either from local grapes or wines or musts imported from other EEC countries. If totally French the wine will be labelled "French table wine". If made from a blend it will be referred to as "a blend of wines from different countries of the EEC". Then again, if it is the result of musts grown elsewhere but vinified in France, the bottle will be labelled "wine made in France from grapes harvested in..."

Most of these vin de table wines are sold under brand names. Though the best can be quite pleasant, it is generally better value to buy a vin de pays. These often cost no more than one of the heavily promoted vin de table brands.

VIN DE PAYS

Vin de pays, which slightly confusingly will also have the words "vin de table" on the label, can only be produced from approved grape varieties in the areas whose name they bear. They are subject to quality testing, and the majority are produced in the hinterland of the French Mediterranean coastal regions.

This system was designed to reward producers prepared to make good wine in the Midi areas of France – where the extra effort is sometimes hardly economic. Many of the robust, lively reds provide excellent value.

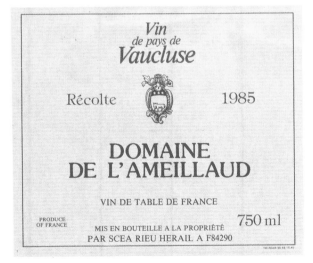

VIN DELIMITE DE QUALITE SUPERIEURE

VDQS wines are produced under the auspices of the *Institut National des Appellations d'Origine*. As the goal of most *viticulteurs* is to achieve AC status, their overall quality is extremely high. Grape variety as well as maximum yield per hectare and methods of cultivation and vinification are closely and legally controlled.

1983

CHATEAU

LES OLLIEUX

75cl

VDQS
LABEL
RN 854

CORBIÈRES

APPELLATION D'ORIGINE VIN DELIMITE DE QUALITE SUPERIEURE

MIS EN BOUTEILLE AU CHATEAU

Mme SURBEZY-CARTIER, PROPRIÉTAIRE A MONTSERET 11200 LEZIGNAN
TÉL. (68) 43.62.61
PRODUIT DE FRANCE

WURMSER

APPELLATION CONTROLEE

The AC system, developed by Baron Le Roy in Châteauneuf-du-Pape in the 'thirties, has a yet stricter production code. These laws concern grape variety, minimum alcoholic content, maximum yield, methods of cultivation, pruning and vinification and, sometimes, even the conditions of storing and ageing.

Just as VDQS wines are entitled to their denomination only after they have satisfied a tasting commission, so wines produced in AC areas can only obtain the "appellation" if they have satisfied all the requirements for that particular region.

The more specific the region designated, the stricter the controls and, therefore, the higher the quality of the wine. For instance, in Bordeaux a wine that carries the general Bordeaux appellation label can come from anywhere in the whole Bordeaux wine producing area. An AC Médoc, on the other hand, must originate from the Médoc region of Bordeaux and an AC Haut Médoc from the superior Haut Médoc area inside the Médoc, while a wine that is AC Pauillac can only have been made in the commune of Pauillac in the Haut Médoc!

There are, however, two exceptions to this rule. In Alsace there is just one appellation for most wines, with *Alsace Grand Cru* designating the superior vineyards. And in Champagne the name alone is regarded as sufficient. There is just one appellation and it is the only AC area which does not have to print the words "Appellation Contrôlée" on its labels.

PRODUIT DE FRANCE

Château de Blomac

MIS EN BOUTEILLE AU CHÂTEAU
Minervois
APPELLATION MINERVOIS CONTROLEE
"CUVÉE TRADITION"
1983
75cl
M. DE THÉLIN – VITICULTEUR A BLOMAC – AUDE

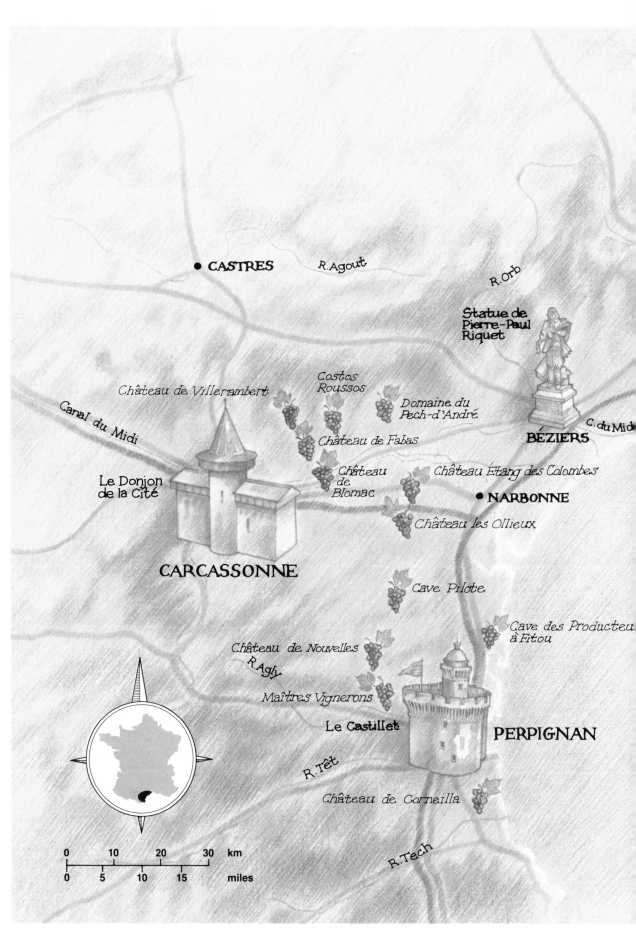

CASTRES

R. Agout

R. Orb

Statue de Pierre-Paul Riquet

Costos Roussos

Château de Villerambert

Domaine du Pech-d'André

Canal du Midi

C. du Midi

BÉZIERS

Château de Fabas

Le Donjon de la Cité

Château Étang des Colombes

Château de Blomac

NARBONNE

Château les Ollieux

CARCASSONNE

Cave Pilote

Cave des Producteurs à Fitou

Château de Nouvelles

R. Agly

Maîtres Vignerons

Le Castillet

PERPIGNAN

R. Têt

Château de Corneilla

R. Tech

| 0 | 10 | 20 | 30 | km |
| 0 | 5 | 10 | 15 | miles |

M. Hérault

Château d'Eau

Domaine de
Mas Combet

Château Flaugergues

MONTPELLIER

• SÈTE

The
LANGUEDOC-
ROUSSILLON
REGION

The historic region of Languedoc-Roussillon basks in the Mediterranean sunshine of the southernmost part of France. Here, the climate is hot, the ground dry and the wine and welcomes plentiful.

In fact, the conditions that prevail in this most prolific wine-producing region – which boasts around 1¼ million acres of grapes – also characterize the wine, which is primarily red and full of warmth and flavour, and the people, whose enjoyment of life is reflected in their hospitality, the wine they drink and the food they eat.

From Nîmes to Perpignan, the countryside changes constantly. Touching the edge of the Massif Central to the north, you'll find sweeping plains filled with vines bordering the coast to the south of Montpellier, while inland the scenery is dramatically different. Here lie the *garrigues* – stony hills covered in scrub, wild flowers and shrubs – that stretch from the lower slopes of the Cèvennes to the foothills of the Pyrénées. This is really Corbières country, proud, defiant and boasting a history of wine-making that goes back some 2,000 years.

To the north, the ancient wine region of Minervois spreads across the sun-soaked land below the Black Mountain. To the south the rugged landscape takes in the region of Roussillon – the last bastion before you reach the Spanish border. This is the home of the famous *vin doux naturel* – the "naturally sweet wine" perfect with desserts or even as an aperitif!

The
LANGUEDOC-ROUSSILLON
REGION

This wine region stretches south of Nîmes to the Spanish border and follows the coastline of the western Mediterranean to the north east beyond Montpellier. Approaching from the routes that follow the lower slopes of the Pyrénées the scenery is dramatic, with soaring mountainous country to the south and the rocky scrubland of the *garrigues* all around you.

Through the forests east of Foix, where a stony outcrop holds an impressive castle, the road to Perpignan leads you through the vineyards of Roussillon. The drive in and out of Tautavel, where the oldest human skull in Europe was found in 1971, is at times breathtaking. Then the land drops away from you, opening out into the plains around Perpignan.

Heading north, you pass through the small vineyards of Fitou, with their delightful full-bodied red wine, and into Corbières. Taking the inland route towards Tuchan and then up through Villeneuve and Durban to the wine centre at Lézignan-Corbières, the roads weave and wend their way through the semi-wild countryside.

Vines will grow anywhere with a south-facing bank to catch the hot Mediterranean sun. This is also hunting country, where the search for the *sanglier* (wild boar) is nothing short of a religion. It certainly makes a delicious dish, accompanied by the local wine.

The land flattens out along the banks of the Aude and, by taking the road across the plains west of the ancient town of Narbonne, you reach Minervois, with Olonzac as its centre. Here again the vines spread for mile after mile, and a tour of the area will take you through some fascinating towns and villages, particularly those on the foot-hills of the Montagne Noir. A trip to Minerve, the tiny historic town tucked into the hillside, from which the region took its name is another must for any visitor. The town was mentioned in the writings of Cicero in 74 BC, and became estalished as a wine centre in the middle ages.

From Narbonne, the roads to the coast take you into the Languedoc and through the vine-yards of La Clape, where you can taste some delicious red wine. Moving on across the open country up through Béziers, a fine hilltop city that dominates the landscape, you will come eventually to the historic capital of Montpellier, with its maze of tiny streets and small squares filled with fascinating shops, restaurants, street cafés and bars.

The land here is green and fertile, with a string of popular beaches and coastal resorts where you can soak up the sun and bathe in the warm Mediterranean water. Inland, too, there are many worthwhile excursions, particularly to the north, following the Hérault river to Ganges and beyond, deep into the heart of the Cévennes. The roads offer magnificent views, as they climb up and along the thickly wooded hillsides, suddenly dropping dramatically down into deep valleys. One of the most rewarding routes takes you west from Nîmes through Ganges and Le Vigan, then across the Massif Central via Saint Affrique to Albi.

REGIONAL SPECIALITIES

The Wines
Languedoc: *Saint Chinian, Saint-Georges-d'Orques, Faugères, La Méjonelle, Clairette du Languedoc, La Clape, Pic-Saint-Louip, Quatourze, Saint-Drégéry, Cabrières, Saint-Christol, Saint-Saturnin, Vérargues, Montpeyroux, Picpoul de Pinet.*
Minervois: *Les Côtes Noires, La Petite Causse, La Clamoux, Le Causse, Les Balcons de l'Aude, Les Mourels, L'Argent Double, Les Serres.*
Corbières/Fitou: *Corbières, Fitou.*
Roussillon: *Côtes du Roussillon, Côtes du Roussillon Villages, Côtes du Roussillon Villages Cavamiany, Côtes du Roussillon*

Latour de France, Rivesaltes, Muscat de Rivesaltes, Maury.

The Food
The traditional country dish is cassoulet, a white bean stew usually made with goose, but pork, mutton and spicy sausages provide more local variations. Saucisses à la Languedocienne, sautéd in goose fat, are also delicious, as is the sanglier (wild boar). There is an interesting selection of country soups, such as oillade (made with pork, potatoes, cabbage and mushrooms) and mourtaîrol (chicken and saffron). Along the coast seafood naturally features

prominently on the menu, with specialities such as cuttlefish in garlic sauce and brandade de morue (salted cod cooked with olive oil and cream).

Left. Dramatic skies brood above this vineyard to the east of Montpellier.
Below. About 50km north-west of Montpellier is the town of Lodeve. The huge cathedral of Saint Fulcran dates back to the 13th century.
Bottom. Traditionally French, a game of boule is enjoyed by the sea at Coullioure, south of Perpignan.

CHATEAU de CORNEILLA
C O R N E I L L A - D E L - V E R C O L

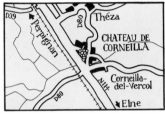

Traditionally, the important wine-growing areas – and particularly Corbières and Roussillon – are dotted with fortified buildings. In years gone by, this part of France was, it seems, perpetually under siege from one intruder or another. It is hardly surprising then that here you will often come across a château in the true sense – built for protection, but also as a centre for wine production.

One such is the Château de Corneilla which stands imposingly on the edge of the village and has a commanding view of the surrounding countryside and the route to Spain. Its history dates back to the time of the Knights Templar in the 12th century.

Philipe Jonquères d'Oriola, the present owner, comes from a family whose origins in this region go back about 500 years. The château itself has 140 hectares, 60 of which are given over to vines. The rest of the land is used for growing cereals, rearing cattle and breeding horses.

Two-thirds of the vines, some of the most southerly in France, produce the AC wines, while the rest go to make

Château de Corneilla, which dates back to the 12th century.

Côtes du Roussillon and vin de table, depending on the quality of the harvest. M. Jonquères is keen to point out that quality is far more important than quantity.

Château de Corneilla
(Philippe Jonquères d'Oriola)
66200 Corneilla-del-Vercol
Telephone: 68 22 05 85

MAITRES VIGNERONS
T A U T A V E L

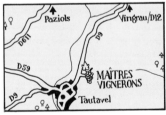

Tautavel has much to recommend itself. The drive to it over the hills from Cases de Pere is quite magnificent. Equally spectacular is the northern route via Vingrau, and discovering the village itself, tucked away in the valley, is an added delight.

The "first man in Europe" was believed to have lived here, though sadly he would not have been able to enjoy the fruits of the vine – as we can be fairly certain that wine was not made 450,000 years ago. In 1964 the first major evidence of "homo-erectus" was discovered by some *vignerons*, and further traces of this important evolutionary link have since been found – the most recent being a skull, excavated in 1983.

All this and much more can be seen in a fascinating museum. And, in keeping with the history of the area, there is another museum which reflects the culture of wine and its production over the centuries. Both are situated close to the *co-opérative* Maîtres Vignerons.

Garrigues – stoney hills – covered with vines, seen from the road to Tautavel near Fitou.

At the *co-opérative's* reception for the *vendange* you can see a computerised control system that handles all the necessary details for each producer. These number nearly 150, who look after the 700 hectares of vines associated with the *co-opérative*.

The success of Maîtres Vignerons, under the direction of Jean-Louis Calvet, is undeniable. Ever since the wine of Côtes du Roussillon Villages was designated as VDQS in 1973, award has followed award.

The resident expert René Renoux, a charming and very knowledgeable guide, will happily show you the various aspects of production once the *vendange* has arrived and will invite you to a little tasting of some of the 14 wines carrying the "Maîtres Vignerons de Tautavel" label.

Maîtres Vignerons
66720 Tautavel
Telephone: 68 29 12 03

CHATEAU de NOUVELLES
TUCHAN

B uried deep in the heart of Hautes Corbières, near the fascinating town of Tuchan, Château de Nouvelles appears like an oasis of wine amid the surrounding rocky terrain.

Turning off the main road, you wind your way up a small valley through semi-mountainous landscape, interrupted only by patches of vines. As you enter the complex of buildings which discreetly hide the winery and a host of surprises, you will find a curiously grand house, tucked in among the trees at the far end. Here, Robert Daurat-Fort lives with his family.

The origins of the property date back to the 12th century, but the only evidence of this is in a 90-foot tower, stone-built and solid, which stands like a sentinel watching over the house. Only crumbling remains of the original fortifications are visible below. If you look up to the top of the tower, you can see a most curious sight – a lone olive tree sprouting from the ancient stone.

M. Daurat-Fort is a commanding figure, warm in his welcome and magnanimous in his hospitality. His estate

Above left. *The imposing, yet elegant, façade of the Château de Nouvelles.*
Above right. *A stone tower is the only surviving remain of the original 12th century property.*

covers some 88 hectares of vines, spread through the valley, which produce an interesting range of very good wine. In fact, there is a fine tradition of wine-production in the family, back through father and son to 1834.

As you enter the winery you are at the top of a steep staircase, from which you get an amazing view of some massive wooden vats. As you reach the bottom, you come to the *dégustation* area – an old *pressoir*. Here, you can sample the delights of M. Daurat-Fort's sweeter wine, served *frais*, or some of the Fitou or Corbières vintages.

Glancing to the left of the old press you can see a sign over the doorway which reads: "*Un repas sans vins est une journée sans soleil.*" (A meal without wine is a day without sun.) Fortunately, here at Château de Nouvelles, there is no problem about enjoying either.

Château de Nouvelles *(Robert Daurat-Fort)*
11350 Tuchan
Telephone: 68 45 40 03

CAVES des PRODUCTEURS à FITOU

F I T O U

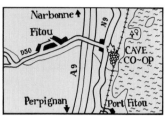

Historically, Fitou boasts some of the longest established red wine of all the appellations from the Languedoc - Roussillon region. The vineyards that produce this unusual wine are contained within two very small areas – one bordering the sea and the other tucked away in the mountainous countryside just inland.

One of the most important producers of this wine is the Caves des Producteurs at Les Cabanes de Fitou, which is most admirably looked after by its president Mme Loubatière. The *co-opérative* has been in existence for more than 30 years, during which time it has not only protected the interests of the smaller growers, but has expanded its production and reputation to offer no less than 10 different wines. The selection available includes the *vin doux naturel* and a range of Corbières wines, since here the two regions overlap. But the Fitou is the wine of which the *co-opérative* is most proud.

The harvest is gathered in each year from approximately 180 different producers, who collectively cultivate 500 hectares of vines. An indication of the degree of selectivity involved, is that production averages about 28 hectolitres per hectare of vine – an unusually low figure for a red wine.

During a visit, you can be sure of a welcome befitting the area. The hospitality is like the wine of Fitou – full-bodied, warm and generous. Tradition plays an important part here and the lasting impressions are of a friendly, efficient *co-opérative*, where the quality of wine is reflected in the quality of the people who make it.

Caves des Producteurs à Fitou
Les Cabanes de Fitou
11510 Fitou
Telephone: 68 45 71 41

CAVE PILOTE

V I L L E N E U V E

Making a surreal landscape, these glass carboys are used to age the Cave Pilote's wine, by exposing it to the rays of the sun.

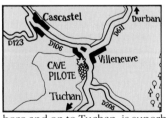

To see an interesting example of wine production, you should certainly visit the Cave Pilote at Villeneuve, a typical Corbières village set in spectacular countryside. The drive alone, here and on to Tuchan, is superb and there's even more to enjoy when you arrive.

Behind the modernized stone-faced frontage lies nearly 40 years of history for this *co-opérative*, which represents more than 80 producers in the Villeneuve area, and covers less than 400 hectares of vines. Here, you will find the full range of wines from the region – including Corbières, Fitou and Rivesaltes.

Under the direction of Michel Nozeran, Cave Pilote has won many awards. Marc Esdamonde, its Maître de Chai, will be happy to show you round the different processes that have helped to earn the Cave's reputation. On your tour you will see the large wooden vats in which the red wine is kept, and the rows of oak barrels used for the best vintages. Another fascinating aspect is the method used to age the *vin doux naturel*. This sweet wine is left under direct sunlight in large glass containers, which look rather like oversized decanters.

Cave Pilote
11360 Villeneuve-Les-Corbières
Telephone: 68 45 91 59

CHATEAU ETANG des COLOMBES
LEZIGNAN-CORBIERES

A vineyard worker tamps down the grapes which are to be transported to the chai.

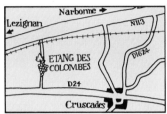

Henri Gualco has plenty to be proud of at Château Etang des Colombes, for here he produces some of the best wine in Corbières. Among many awards he has received, few could have given him more pleasure than the Gold Medallion for his 1981 red wine, awarded at the prestigious Concours des Vins de Mâcon.

M. Gualco owns a most pleasing property. The house dates back to the 17th century and M. Gualco is of the third generation of *vignerons* to produce wine here. He looks after 110 hectares, 72 of which are taken up by the vineyard where 10 different types of grape are cultivated.

M. Gualco's love for tradition is nowhere better reflected than in the *cave de dégustation*, which is in fact a wine museum. One of the most impressive exhibits is a late 19th century steam engine, designed by a Benoit Raclet. This was used to make hot water to spray vines infected by the *pyrale* – a caterpillar which ate its way through the crop, creating havoc with the harvest. This problem reached its peak before the phylloxera almost wiped out France's wine industry.

The full range of production at Château Etang des Colombes includes red, white and rosé wines. The growth of the business has brought with it the need to expand the facilities, and M. Gualco has just had an underground *cave* built alongside the main buildings. This and the other interesting areas of production ensure a visit to remember – and the museum is a special bonus.

Château Etang des Colombes (*Henri Gualco*)
11200 Lézignan-Corbières
Telephone: 68 27 00 03

CHATEAU les OLLIEUX
MONTSERET

When her husband died, Françoise Surbézy-Cartier was left with the task of keeping on Château les Ollieux. This was a considerable challenge – not least in maintaining the 53 hectares of vines that make up the wine-growing part of this impressive property. Not only did Mme Surbézy-Cartier face up to the challenge, but she also made sure that the château's reputation grew accordingly. Among the many awards she has won for her red and rosé wines since 1978, are gold medals from no lesser Concours than Paris and Mâcon.

Thus tradition has been admirably upheld, since wine-making has been very much in the family blood since 1855. The history of the vines at Château les Ollieux goes back further than this, since some existed around the property as long ago as the early 14th century. Records also show that in 1153 the buildings were used as a Cistercian Abbey.

In keeping with the approach she takes to her work and her wine, Mme Surbézy-Cartier offers a friendly welcome in the *salle de dégustation*. Here, you can appreciate the many honours bestowed on her wine, while testing the reasons why.

Château les Ollieux (*Mme Surbézy-Cartier*)
Montséret
11200 Lézignan-Corbières
Telephone: 68 43 32 61

CHATEAU de FABAS

L A U R E

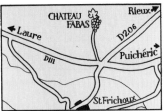

The walls of Château de Fabas enclose much Minervois history. The property was originally a fortified farm dating back to the 16th century. It has survived remarkably well and there is still much to see of the old walls and towers within this curious but interesting mixture of architectural styles.

You approach the château down a long drive lined with conifers which passes through the 57 hectares of vineyards. On arrival, you will be welcomed by Jean-Pierre Ormieres or his wife, who live in and work this interesting property. M. Ormieres, a quiet and pleasant man, takes his responsibility as a *viticulteur* very seriously, producing some very good red, rosé and, he admits, a little white as well.

M. Ormieres' quest for the continued quality and reputation of his wine has brought him to experiment with oak barrels in which to age the red. The wine will stay in the casks for approximately two years before it is bottled. He also allows each *cépage* to ferment separately, in order to determine the final quality more accurately and, therefore, to judge the best proportions in which the blend the different grapes.

In 1829, Château de Fabas was one of the largest vineyards in the region, covering some 330 hectares. The Ormieres have an antique plan of the original estate at that date. The present family, which has lived here for three generations since the 1930s, owns a considerably reduced area, although M. Ormieres is continually replanting and increasing production as and when he can.

Visitors are welcome to the *chai* and the *caveau de dégustation*, set in the far corner of the courtyard. Tasting is carried out among some of the old wooden barrels kept there.

Château de Fabas (*Jean-Pierre Ormieres*)
11800 Laure-Minervois
Telephone: 68 78 17 82

CHATEAU de VILLERAMBERT

C A U N E S

Entering the gateway of this walled château, you cannot help feeling that it is a noble place. There is a lot of history here, and traditions are still maintained, because the owner Marceau Moureau still believes in their importance.

Like other well-established châteaux, Château de Villerambert did not remain unscathed by the vicissitudes of history. But one family survived over many turbulent years to continue the traditions. This was the family of Vernon, whose descendants kept possession of Villerambert for over 400 years – from 1395 to 1825.

For six generations since then, the ancestors of the present owner have lived and worked with the vines, producing wine of very high quality. Fortunately, this is guaranteed for at least another generation, since M. Moureau's son has been studying the noble culture of wine-making and now works alongside his father. The father and son team look after the 100 or so hectares that belong to this vineyard and a nearby property – Château Villegly.

M. Moureau is proud to show you round the extensive buildings, including the *cave* and *chai* and then take you into the château's dungeon for a little taste! There's no fear of being kept there though, except perhaps to prolong the *dégustation*. The dungeon is a fascinating feature that naturally appeals to visitors. It is sobering, however, to remind onself that earlier visitors were not so fortunate!

Château de Villerambert (*Marceau Moureau*)
11160 Caunes-Minervois
Telephone: 68 26 40 26

Above right. *The evening sun lights a rocky Minervois landscape.*
Right. *Marceau Moreau presides over the dégustation in the Château de Villerambert's dungeon.*

COSTOS ROUSSOS

TRAUSSE

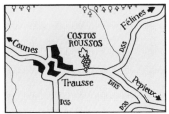

Vine growers do not always live in their vineyards. Their homes are elsewhere, possibly in the nearby village, and the vines may well only be tended at weekends. This is certainly the case at Trausse, a quaint old village in the true Minervois tradition. Out of about 200 producers attached to the Costos Roussos co-opérative, only a dozen or so actually live where they work. This does not appear to pose any major problems, however, and certainly makes no noticeable difference to the quality of the wines produced. The total area of vines involved is around 650 hectares.

Under the control of its young director, Michel Philippe, the co-opérative works happily and successfully – as it has done for well over 50 years. And a visit here is particularly rewarding for a taste of the "old" red wine. In the Minervois region, this means one that's drunk possibly eight or ten years after the harvest.

The visitor is welcome to look round the winery and the different areas of production. One interesting feature is the storage of the oak barrels on three levels, which are connected by an iron staircase at one end. Here the pleasant red Minervois wine matures before being bottled.

Costos Roussos
11160 Trausse-Minervois
Telephone: 68 78 31 15

Costos Roussos – the co-opérative winery at the quaint old village of Trausse.

DOMAINE du PECH-d'ANDRE

AZILLANET

The Domaine du Pech-d'André is pleasantly situated just off the road from Olonzac to the hills of Minervois. It is en route to the ancient and fascinating village of Minerve, which is also well worth visiting. The house stands on rising ground, ("pech" means a small hill), and you approach the property along a drive lined with olive trees. All around are the vines that make up the 30 hectares which the Remaury family tend with great care.

The estate was in the André family for some 300 years and has been run for the last 20 years by Marc Remaury and his wife Germaine. They are a quiet, pleasant couple who will happily show you round and explain about Pech-d'André and its wine. Inside, the main part of the winery is kept immaculately clean and there is a delightfully atmos-

The stony soil typical of the region looks an unlikely supporter of plant-life, but the vines thrive at M. Remaury's domaine.

pheric small *cave* behind the reception area, which has a floor of pebbles. All the facilities are situated neatly below the house.

About two-thirds of the vineyard contains the *cépages* that make the AC wine for which the Domaine boasts such a good reputation. These are planted on land facing south, fully exposed to the hot Mediterranean sun, for it is the warmth from this that helps perfect the quality of the wine.

Domaine du Pech-d'André (Marc Remaury)
34210 Azillanet
Telephone: 68 91 22 66

CHATEAU de BLOMAC

B L O M A C

One of the largest wine - producing properties in Minervois, Château de Blomac dominates the small village of the same name of which it is the centrepiece. Its importance is not only reflected in its position, but also by the quality of wine it produces.

This imposing château is not as old as you might think, having been built after the French Revolution in the early years of the 19th century. In about 1825 the owner of the time, Baron de Rolland Trassenel, created the impressive *chai* behind the chapel, which makes a curious neighbour. The main features of the *chai* are the roof, where you can admire some magnificent timbers, and the rows of large wooden vats in which the wine is kept before being bottled.

The vines, which surround the village, cover some 115 hectares. Roughly one third of these produce the AC wine for which Château de Blomac has justly earned many awards. The present owner is Jean de Thélin, a constantly busy man who organises a local *viticulteurs* group for the promotion of wine from that area. His family has lived and

The village chapel at Blomac, a curious neighbour for the winery.

worked on the estate for more than 50 years.

M. de Thélin employs about 15 people through the year – with 30 or so extra pairs of hands during the *vendange*. Although about two-thirds of the vines are harvested by machine, there are still very many to be picked by hand.

Château de Blomac (Jean de Thélin)
11700 Caperdu
Telephone: 68 79 01 54

CHATEAU FLAUGERGUES

M O N T P E L L I E R

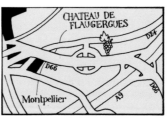

For a château built before the Revolution to have remained untouched by history's ravages is remarkable. For one to have been preserved as completely as Château Flaugergues has, is verging on the incredible. This fine example of late 17th century architecture stands majestically on the hillside to the west of Montpellier, and is protected from the sight of some unfortunate new developments by a cluster of trees. Despite the years that have passed since the château was built in 1690 by its imaginative creator Etienne de Flaugergues, much is as it must have been nearly 300 years

There is nothing understated about the majestic 17th century Château Flaugergues.

The Cirque de Navacelles – a vast crater formed by the erosive action of the winding river Vis. This scenic spectacular is situated about 55km north-west of Montpellier.

ago. Also remarkable is the fact that it stayed in the same family all this time. The present owner, Comte Henri de Colbert, is a friendly, energetic man who is very proud of his inheritance.

Entering the grounds, along one of several tree-lined avenues that run up to the main buildings, you come to the complex below the château, bordering a large courtyard. This looks more like a stable block than the heart of the wine production – but don't be fooled. The vineyard spreads round the château, covering some 33 hectares, and apart from the various other features such as the *cave* and *chai*, there is a well-stocked *salle de dégustation*. Here, as well as tasting the delights of the red, rosé and white wines, you can feast yourself on a whole range of local products, including wine from other vineyards and a selection of the region's culinary delights.

Climbing the steps that weave their way up from the far corner of the courtyard, you reach the château's terraced garden. From here you can get the best view of the château's elegant façade, with its ballustrade, and the statues at either side of the main entrance. Some of the rooms are also open to visitors. Main features include a magnificent three-tiered staircase, some Brussels tapestries and other interesting furnishing and furniture.

Château Flaugergues (*Comte Henri de Colbert*)
1744 Route de Maugio
34000 Montpellier
Telephone: 67 65 51 72

DOMAINE de MAS COMBET

M A U G I O

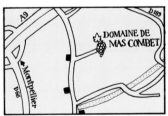

In complete contrast to the grandeur of Château Flaugergues, a few kilometres away there is a small property where a family named Gilles cultivates some 6 hectares of vines. Away from the noise and traffic of the Autoroute Languedocienne, on a stretch of exposed ground, Paul Gilles has, with his father and mother, recently started up in business.

Until 1978 the grapes from the vineyard of Domaine de Mas Combet went, with those of other small-scale *viticulteurs*, to the local *co-opérative*. However, Paul's father decided to start making and bottling his own wine. There was, of course, much work to be done and expensive equipment to buy. The objective was to establish a reputation for AC wine – and this was achieved in 1985 with the *domaine's* red vintage.

You will find visiting this small, homely vineyard a refreshing contrast to the refined, large-scale operations of more established and privileged producers. Paul Gilles is well aware of the huge challenge that faces the family. He modestly accepts the progress so far made and is quietly confident of further success.

Naturally, he welcomes visitors to the *cave* and will happily show you round the vines, explaining in detail

each type of grape, the terrain and other conditions that go to make some very enjoyable wine.

Domaine de Mas Combet (*Paul Gilles*)
34130 Maugio
Telephone: 67 29 32 70

Above left. The cave at the Domaine de Mas Combet.
Above right. As at most wineries, you can buy wine "on tap". Bottles are probably easier for visitors to transport home.

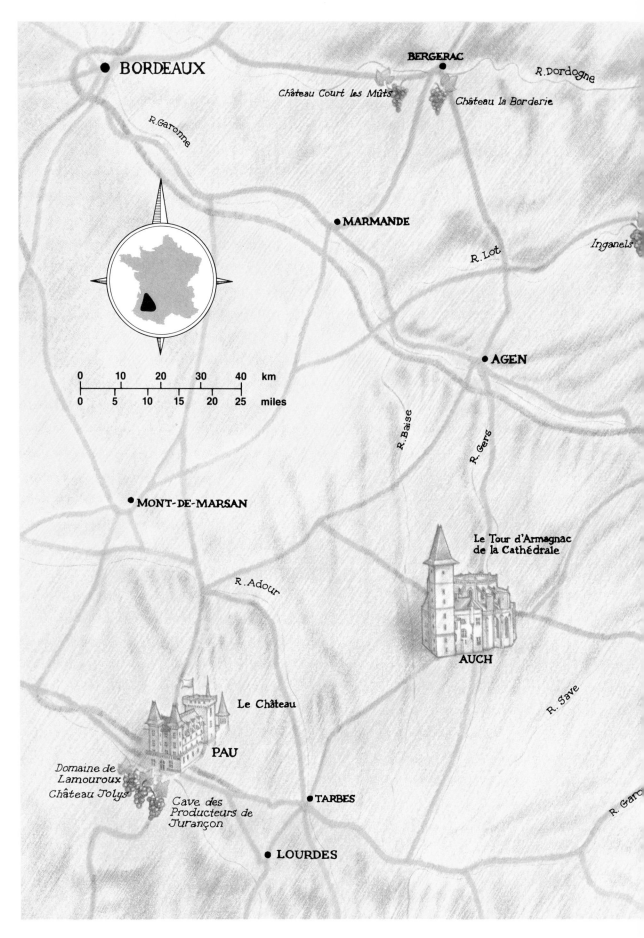

● BORDEAUX

BERGERAC

R. Dordogne

Château Court les Mûts

Château la Borderie

R. Garonne

● MARMANDE

R. Lot

Inganels

● AGEN

R. Baise

R. Gers

● MONT-DE-MARSAN

Le Tour d'Armagnac
de la Cathédrale

R. Adour

AUCH

R. Save

Le Château

PAU

Domaine de
Lamouroux
Château Jolys

● TARBES

R. Garo

Cave des
Producteurs de
Jurançon

● LOURDES

0   10   20   30   40   km

0   5   10   15   20   25   miles

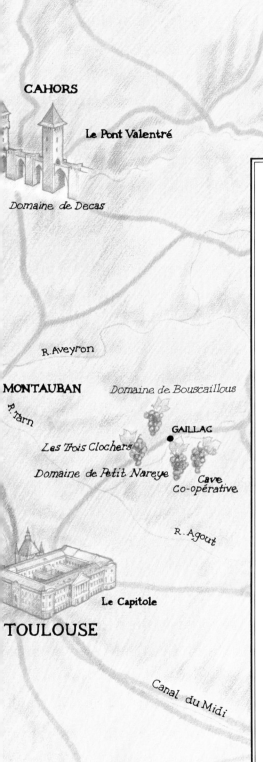

CAHORS

Le Pont Valentré

Domaine de Decas

R. Aveyron

MONTAUBAN

Domaine de Bouscaillous

R. Tarn

GAILLAC

Les Trois Clochers

Domaine de Petit Nareye

Cave
Co-opérative

R. Agout

Le Capitole

TOULOUSE

Canal du Midi

The SUD-OUEST

REGION

his delightfully varied region spreads across the south-west corner of France, inland from Bordeaux and south to the Pyrénées. It is made up of a collection of small wine areas, in total covering some 50,000 acres of grapes. Each area has its own special character, its own wines.

As is the case elsewhere in the country, France's mighty rivers provide the focal points for much of this spectacular region – the Dordogne flowing through Bergerac, the Lot through Cahors, the Tarn through Gaillac and the Gave de Pau and the Gave d'Oloron to the north and south of Jurançon.

The landscape of the wine areas shows a dramatic contrast from the north to the south of the region. There are gently rolling plains around Bergerac with orchards and tobacco fields, while in the mountainous region around Cahors, the countryside is full of reminders of its pre-Renaissance history, abounding with castles, fortified manor houses and churches.

Below Cahors are the green hillside vineyards of Gaillac, and to the east the ancient city of Albi. To the north-west of the region lie the small wine areas of Duras and Marmandais, with Fronton to the north of Toulouse.

To the north of Armagnac country the small vineyards of Buzet lie amid orchards and farmland, while on the southern edge of the area are the hillside vines of Madiran, on the left bank of the Adour.

The
SUD-OUEST
REGION

This region includes some of the prettiest and most spectacular landscapes in this part of France and is also of considerable historic interest. The classic medieval cities of Bergerac, Cahors and Albi, for example, provide fine spectacles for the visitor. This is a countryside full of fine castles, churches, museums and bridges as well as productive vineyards.

Bergerac is an excellent starting point for the tourist. It is a town full of antiquity – fine churches, fascinating museums, narrow cobbled streets and impressive architecture. The vines lie mainly to the south and west, with Monbazillac and its elegant château proudly boasting the famous sweet wine of the same name.

To the south-west you can enjoy the fresh, light wines of Duras produced around the old market town. The château commands a magnificent view of the surrounding countryside towards Marmande, yet another of the region's scattered vineyards, and Buzet, west of Agen.

Travelling inland following the course of the river Lot, you reach the medieval city of Cahors. Here, the riverside scenery is dominated by the beautiful fortified 14th century Pont Valentré, with its three magnificent towers. The vineyards stretch along the banks of the Lot and up over the hillsides beyond the city.

Heading south towards Toulouse you will find the small vineyards of Fronton. And to the south-east of

Toulouse is Gaillac, where you can enjoy some of the celebrated sparkling white wines and stand on the bridge overlooking the Abbaye Saint-Michel. Up river is the tourist centre of Albi, an historic city with a magnificent cathedral and quaint narrow streets. Heading south-west, do make a slight detour into Lisle-sur-Tarn, a delightful curiosity with its unusual town square and narrow streets.

Through the sprawling city of Toulouse and continuing south-west, you reach Armagnac country. En route to Pau you pass the vineyard of Madiran and to the west you can discover the little known wines of Béarn. But the most important vineyards are just a few miles to the south of Pau. Here, the delightful wines of Jurançon are produced from the terraces of vines that climb the foothills of the Pyrénées.

The scenery here is nothing short of magnificent – in either direction. But taking the road east towards Languedoc-Roussillon and the Mediterranean brings rich reward. If you have a good head for heights, take the route that traverses the Col du Tourmalet. At well over 6,000 feet at its summit, the view on a clear day is breaktaking. The road to the Mediterranean continues along the foothills of the Pyrénées, up hillsides, down valleys, through forest and woodland, eventually opening out into a spectacular panorama around Quillan on the edge of Corbières country.

REGIONAL SPECIALITIES

The Wines
Major types: *Bergerac, Monbazillac, Montravel, Pécharmant, Rosette, Côtes de Saussignac, Côtes de Duras, Cahors, Côtes de Fronton, Gaillac, Jurançon, Côtes de Buzet, Côtes du Marmandais, Irouléguy.*

The Food
Here in the Sud-Ouest, the food is as rich and varied as the countryside. Ranging from the traditional truffles, confit de canard (preserved duck) and foie gras from Périgord in the north to the cassoulet (stew) or garbure (soup) found around the Pyrénées in the south. As well as pork, goose and duck, the northern region enjoys walnuts, peaches and plums in a variety of

desserts. To the east you can enjoy the world famous Roquefort cheese from the Massif Central, while among many tasty dishes there is poulet aux girolles (chicken

with chanterelles mushrooms). Navette Albigeoise (almond and orange cake) and prunes in red wine are particularly delicious regional desserts.

Top. An eerie glow is created by early morning mist in Monbazillac.

Above. This antique alembic ambulant (a travelling still) is a vanishing feature of Armagnac. No longer horse drawn, stills convert white wine made from Baco and Ugni Blanc grapes into Armagnac brandy.

Left. Bloodless bullfights, Courses Landaises, are common in the Landes area around the town of Pau. The matador's skill lies in leaving his escape from the path of the charging bull as late as possible.

CHATEAU COURT les MUTS
S A U S S I G N A C

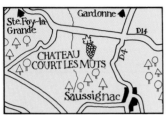

Château Court les Mûts, which nestles against the hillside to the west of Bergerac in the area of Saussignac, has a very modern feel. Far from putting you off, however, this aspect offers its own particular interest and appeal. Indeed, the friendly atmosphere that greets you as you drive up through the neat rows of vines is further extended by Pierre Sadoux and his charming wife.

Not only does M. Sadoux make wine but he also tests it, in his role as the local wine analyst, and his expertise in this area will make itself evident as you wander round the vineyard, *cave* and small museum.

In stark contrast to the almost clinical appearance of the wine-storing area which contains the vats, and the long gallery with a row of brand new oak casks, you will find an intersting range of historical items on display. These include farming implements and cooper's tools – for making barrels.

You are also invited to inspect M. Sadoux's laboratory. Here, row after row of small bottles represent the labours of the neighbouring *viticulteurs* and contain samples of wine from throughout the area, brought in for M. Sadoux's official inspection.

The speciality of the area is the sweet dessert wine of Saussignac, where this vineyard is situated. It is recommended to be sampled with that Perigordian delicacy *foie gras*. The other wines produced here are those traditional to the region – Bergerac red, white and rosé.

Château Court les Mûts (Pierre Sadoux)
Razac de Saussignac
24240 Sigoulès
Telephone: 53 27 92 17

The Place Cayla in Bergerac. The Maison du Vin *is on the right.*

CHATEAU la BORDERIE
M O N B A Z I L L A C

The scenery around Bergerac is, almost without exception, a continuous spread of vineyards, as row after row of vines carpet the plain around this famous town and reach up the hillsides to the south. Below the impressive landmark of the Château Monbazillac grow the grapes from which the famous sweet white wine of the same name is made.

One of the largest of the vineyards here is the Château la Borderie which, in conjunction with the smaller Château du Treuil de Nailhac, covers some 73 hectares. Together, they produce around 4,000 hectolitres of wine each year, of which there are always some 300,000 bottles in stock. Apart from the sweet Monbazillac white, the Château la Borderie also produces the traditional Bergerac red, white and rosé wines.

The property has been in M. Vidal's family for four generations and while there is scope in the area to produce more of the sweet Monbazillac wine, M. Vidal explains

Above. M. Vidal's Château la Borderie – one of the largest vineyards in the area.

Right. Château Monbazillac, and vines from which the sweet white wine is made.

that new outlets need to be found. As it is, he is increasing his production of red wine, where the market is considerably more lucrative.

As you drive in to this delightful château, you are assured of a friendly welcome. And should you take children you can leave them playing happily on the front lawn, where swings and a slide are provided to enable you to enjoy the tour and *dégustation* in peace. You can see the very latest in wine pressing and filtration equipment, and sample the full range of refreshing local wine.

Château la Borderie (M. Vidal)
Monbazillac
2420 Sigoulès
Telephone 53 57 00 36

INGANELS
PUY-L'EVEQUE

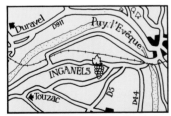

Travelling west from Cahors you will come to the pretty town of Puy-L'Evêque, built on the side of a hill running down to the banks of the Lot, an impressive river that dominates this wine-growing valley. Lying a few kilometres to the south, on the other side of the railway line, is Inganels – the vineyard of Jean Galbert. The friendly M. Galbert owns 12 hectares of vines, most of which had to be replaced in 1956 after a severe February frost destroyed much of the stock.

Despite the quiet, peaceful and homely atmosphere that greets you on your arrival at the *cave*, the vineyard itself is efficiently run and employs many modern production techniques. According to M. Galbert, up to 80% of wine producers in the region now use machines to pick the grapes, but whereas most are part-owners of a picking machine, he has his own. During the guided tour round the *cave*, your host will be happy to explain the wine-making process in detail, even down to the special chemical earth compound called Diatomite, through which the wine is filtered to remove impurities.

M. Galbert stores his Cahors wine for two years in the concrete vats before bottling it. Then the wine is kept in large wooden crates, each containing 600 bottles. In recent years M. Galbert has won many awards for his wine. The certificates which provide the evidence are proudly displayed in the entrance to the *cave*.

Inganels (Jean Galbert)
46700 Puy-L'Evêque
Telephone: 65 21 32 64

DOMAINE de DECAS

T R E S P O U X

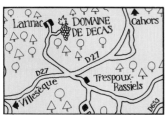

L eaving the bustling town of Cahors to the south-west via the magnificent 14th century Pont Valentré, the road climbs quite steeply at times up the side of the valley on to semi-mountainous terrain. Then, suddenly, it flattens out and you will find yourself in more traditional vineyard territory. Here, you'll discover the home and vineyard of Robert Decas and his family in the hamlet of Lannac, on the outskirts of the old village of Trespoux.

Although the size of the vineyard may look modest, M. Decas is dedicated to his work and the quality of his wine is excellent. The wine is produced in the building adjacent to the 400-year-old house which includes a small *cave* dating back to the 13th century. Dusty bottled samples of previous vintages are stored at one end of the *cave* while several large wooden casks dominate the cool stone room at the other end.

The vineyard, which stretches over some 6 hectares, has been in the Decas family for four generations, ever since the dreaded phylloxera devastated the French wine industry in the 1860s. M. Decas replanted his vines in 1963 to ensure the wine's excellent quality was maintained.

Modern technology has not completely taken over the

Landscape near Cahors – a magnificent view.

Its balcony decked with flowers, the 400-year-old Domaine de Decas basks in the southern sun.

traditional processes in the wine industry – and certainly not as far as M. Decas is concerned. He insists that there are still some jobs, such as grape picking, that are best done by hand. He believes that too many foreign bodies find their way into the wine when machines are used.

M. Decas leaves the wine to age in his concrete vat for at least two years. During this time, samples are taken for analysis to check on the strength and quality.

Domaine de Decas (*Robert Decas et Fils*)
Trespoux-Rosseils
46090 Cahors
Telephone: 65 35 37 74

DOMAINE des BOUSCAILLOUS

M O N T E L S

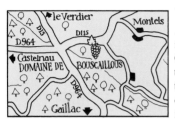

Local tradition fortunately dies hard up in the hillsides above Gaillac, and nowhere in the region is this more true than at the Domaine des Bouscaillous. This relatively small, but significant, vineyard nestles comfortably in the folding landscape, and offers quite dramatic views of both the high ground and the valley below, with the River Tarn meandering through. Here, Yvon and Monique Maurel look after 16 hectares of vines which produce some of the best wine in the area.

M. Maurel has tried using a machine for harvesting, but wasn't happy with the results, so he returned to the traditional method of hand-picking. During the *vendange*, he employs up to a dozen extra pairs of hands.

At Bouscaillous, the vineyard is very much a family affair – going back four generations. M. Maurel is proud of his home and his vines, as a visit will quickly bear out. Production is carried out on a traditional basis and the visitor can look around and then taste the wine in the clean and compact *cave* behind the house.

The Maurels have other business interests besides wine. There is some camping "*à la ferme*" (on the farm) and Monique exploits her culinary skills by producing Confits d'Oie, Foie d'Oie and Graisse d'Oie for sale.

Domaine des Bouscaillous (*Yvon Maurel*)
Montels
81140 Castelnau-de-Montmiral
Telephone: 63 33 18 85

Madame Mourel at home in the delightful setting of the Domaine des Bourscaillous in the hills above Gaillac.

LES TROIS CLOCHERS

S A I N T - S A L V Y - d e - C O U F E N S

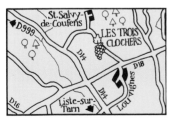

From Gaillac, the drive to Les Trois Clochers takes you through the countryside west of the town of Saint-Salvy-l'Eglise, following the contours of the hills to the north.

There's a friendly country welcome awaiting your arrival at the vineyard, for the people who produce the wine sold under this label all come from the countryside around Gaillac. The three belltowers after which this vineyard is named form part of the neighbouring landscape, with the main *cave* being situated below the most westerly tower.

Les Trois Clochers is a mini *co-opérative*. Since 1967 three *viticulteurs* – Jean Fonvieille, Louis Pradel and Yves Pages – have combined their talents and resources to produce the full range of Gaillac wines. Fine examples they are too, as the 22 gold medals won since 1971 indicate.

This set-up is a prime example of friends joining forces to improve their wine and compete more successfully in a demanding market. And the visitor can share the "*joie de vivre*" that certainly helps motivate the three men.

Les Trois Clochers
Saint-Salvy-de-Coufens
81310 Lisle sur Tarn
Telephone: 63 57 34 04

DOMAINE de PETIT NAREYE

C A D A L E N

Don't be misled by the name of the vineyard, since the Rotier family who owns the Domaine de Petit Nareye has anything but small ideas when it comes to making wine. When I visited the *domaine* there were some 20 hectares of vines, but the family was planning to expand this over the following years. In fact they had just started their own bottling – an important step on the road to becoming a substantial wine producer.

Petit Nareye is interesting for several reasons. It is a delightful property, set in the green rolling countryside near Gaillac, on the south side of the River Tarn. It is also

These geese will no doubt meet their end in some of the Sud-Ouest's famed foie gras *dishes.*

easy to see that it is industrious and efficient, run principally by father and son.

It hasn't taken Gerard Rotier and his son Alain long to earn a reputation for making good red wine. M. Rotier bought the property in 1974, since when he has replanted the vines. He began by selling his grapes to the local *co-opérative* in Técou, but with Alain's serious involvement in the business over the last few years, the decision was taken to actually make wine at Petit Nareye.

There's a simple but pleasant reception and tasting area in front of the *chai* and, with the friendly, open welcome you can expect here, a visit to Petit Nareye is a most refreshing experience.

Domaine de Petit Nareye
(Gerard and Alain Rotier)
Cadalen
81600 Gaillac
Telephone: 63 41 75 14

CAVE CO-OPERATIVE
T E C O U

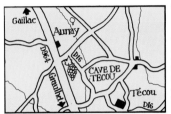

To understand the role that the Cave Co-opérative at Técou plays in the production of a full range of Gaillac wines, you need to know how vineyards are organized in this small, but significant region. Unlike the grand châteaux of Bordeaux, where it is not unusual to find vineyards of 50 to 100 hectares, Gaillac is primarily a region of small, but well-organized growers. Hence, the *co-opérative* represents 450 producers, covering an area of some 700 hectares, so you can see that the average individual vineyard size is very small indeed.

Under the efficient direction of Alain Boutrit, the associated winegrowers of this pleasant region live with the assurance that their future is in good hands. They do not have to invest in costly equipment or worry about where to sell, as all this is looked after by the *co-opérative*.

The guided tour of Técou will take you round all stages of production at the winery, which looks quite factory-like. But when you're producing some 55,000 hectolitres a year, that's hardly surprising.

Quality control is, of course, of prime importance. Checks are made at various stages in the growth of each producer's vines, as well as those carried out throughout production. What is not up to AC standard will end up as Vin de Pays

Michel Sirvon presides over the dégustation *at the Cave de Tecou, where a fine glass of Gaillac wine is guaranteed.*

des Côtes du Tarn or Vin de Table.

A look at a video film made by the *co-opérative* certainly helps you to understand more about the wines of this region. Then you can sample a selection at the *dégustation* and reception areas, courtesy of M. Michel Sirvon.

Cave de Técou
Técou
81600 Gaillac
Telephone: 63 33 00 80

CAVE des PRODUCTEURS de JURANCON
G A N

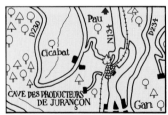

In Gan, at the Cave des Producteurs, more than 300 producers bring the *vendange* from 400 hectares of vines to be made into the best quality wine possible each year. Founded in 1949 by Frederic Miramon, the *cave* has done much over the years to encourage the prosperity of vineyards and enhance the reputation of Jurançon's wine.

By the standards of some other wine-producing regions, the Cave des Producteurs is not massive. Nevertheless there is much to see and much to impress – not least the range of fascinating wines. At the time of my visit, the *cave* was producing some million and a half bottles a year. This is made up of 10,000 hectolitres of dry white wine from the Gros Manseng grape, and 3,000 hectolitres of sweet white wine from the Petit Manseng.

A trip round the *cave* will show the visitor old and new methods working together. Traditional methods of vinification are used here, with the aid of some of the latest equipment – including a bank of stainless steel fermentation tanks situated alongside the railway line behind the *cave*.

One plus point for the visitor is that you can see all of the central pressing area from several vantage points above the impressive machinery. There is a special reception area too, where you can taste and enjoy the range of good wines.

Caves des Producteurs de Jurançon
53, Avenue Henri IV
64290 Gan
Telephone: 59 21 57 03

CHATEAU JOLYS

G A N · J U R A N C O N

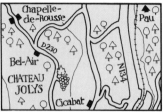

All impressions gained from Château Jolys lead the visitor to the conclusion that it has indeed been aptly named! Set high up in the hills above Jurançon, on the Route des Vins, Château Jolys – the elegant home of the Latrille family – dominates the surrounding countryside.

Pierre-Yves Latrille is president of the Syndicat de Défense des Vins de Jurançon, a responsibility he takes very seriously. Indeed, M. Latrille is very much a father figure in the region, which he moved to from Algeria in 1958. His experience as a wine producer was gained in Algeria and the results of his labours on this once run-down property bear witness to his skills.

The wine produced at the château is all white. Two-thirds of the château's 30 hectares of vines are Gros Manseng. These have large grapes which produce a dry white wine. The rest is the small variety, rich in sugar, which produces a sweet white wine. The *vendange* is all carried out by hand in this part of France as the ground can be very steep indeed.

Although M. Latrille has not got a separate reception and tasting area, he hopes to create one before too long. However, there is much of interest for the visitor to look at in the *cave* and tasting the delightful wine is also a pleasure.

M. Latrille is above all else a working *propriétaire*, but is is well worth seeing if he'll spend the time to discuss the area, the wine and the people – for whom he has a great affection. Here is a fine example of the gentleman *viticulteur*, with perhaps a touch of the English in him. Maybe that's

because, as he says, he was introduced to tea-drinking in Algeria during the Second World War, when his property was used as barracks for the British Army's Royal Engineers. However, the welcome you will receive here is most definitely in the best of French traditions.

Château Jolys *(Pierre-Yves Latrille)*
64290 Gan
Telephone: 59 21 72 79

Above. *The impressive Château Jolys dominates the hilly countryside above Gan.*
Below. *The Cirque de Gavarnie, a vast panorama of mountains high in the Pyrénées, is about 50km south of Lourdes.*

DOMAINE de LAMOUROUX

L A C H A P E L L E D E R O U S S E

The compact region of Jurançon is set in the steep hillside south of Pau, with the mighty Pyrénées beyond. When you see the landscape, you realise why most of the producers supply direct to the *co-opérative*. With very few hectares of vines apiece, producing and bottling wine at each vineyard is out of the question.

However, there are a few independent *viticulteurs* here and you could do no better than to call at the Domaine de Lamouroux. This is tucked away near the tiny village of La Chapelle de Rousse, in the heart of the Jurançon region. Here, with the help of his son-in-law Richard Ziemek and other members of the family, M. Jean Chigé has overcome the problems posed by the landscape and successfully produces wine from his 6 hectares of vines.

The property, which dates back more than 200 years,

Sunflowers meet vines, in this scene near the town of Pau.

came into the family when M. Chigé's grandfather bought it in 1890. Born and bred here, M. Chigé and his father before him have continued the family tradition. Today the vineyard produces some 30,000 bottles of wine each year. A little extra help is needed during the *vendange*, but otherwise the property is run very much by the family, who are happy to welcome any visitor.

Your visit will take in the various areas of production and one interesting feature to look out for is the old wine press. Nowadays, modern technology has largely taken over, but one or two pairs of feet have been known to help out on occasions!

Domaine de Lamouroux
(Jean Chigé and Richard Ziemek)
La Chapelle de Rousse
64110 Jurançon
Telephone: 59 21 74 41

BUYING WINE

If, when you're deciding which wine to buy, you only want a few bottles for immediate drinking, there is little problem. The complications arise when you decide to buy in larger quantities – perhaps to start your own cellar.

BUYING IN FRANCE

It may *seem* cheaper to buy wine in bulk containers and ship it back home to bottle yourself. But remember, even if the import duty is no problem, bottling wine of any quality is a risky business. By buying wine in bottles you can be assured that it will retain its quality.

If the wine you fancy is young, and needs several years to mature, you may find that the grower or merchant is prepared to store it for you and ship it at a later date.

BUYING AT HOME

If you are looking for large quantities of wine the choices are:
A good wine merchant: These provide an individual service and many sell recent vintages of fine wine which can be delivered when they mature. Increasingly, the largest also offer a mail-order service.
A wine club: A good way to try a large selection of wine as most will allow you to purchase mixed cases and thus taste a wider variety.

A wine auction: Probably only for the confident wine buyer. It is always best to attend pre-sale tastings – a useful education in themselves. Also calculate the commission, tax and any duty payable before you bid.

ASSESSMENT

The most important aspect of wine – taste – is also the most subjective. Despite what "experts" might say, some people actually *prefer* a young beaujolais to a mature claret. If you take every opportunity to taste as many wines as possible, you will begin to recognise the characteristics you find most attractive. Whether you are tasting in your own home or in the cellar of a French grower, there are certain basic qualities to judge.

Look at the wine to assess its clarity, depth of colour, sparkle (or lack of it) and viscosity.

Smell is most important. How fruity is the bouquet? Is it complex or straightforward? Are there traces of any other aromas, such as yeast, wood or chemicals?

Finally *taste* the wine to assess its sweetness, acidity, "body" (or "weight in the mouth"), flavour, length of time the taste lingers and its tannin level. The tannin, which tastes not unlike cold tea, can be the most difficult to assess. If the wine you are tasting is for immediate drinking then there is no problem, since the tannin level should be balanced and pleasant. If, on the other hand, you are tasting this year's vintage claret, particularly one of the better ones, the tannin content can be overpowering and the subtleties of the wine will only become apparent with practice.

FOOD AND WINE

Finally, what wine should accompany what food? There are no hard and fast rules that *have* to be obeyed, so drink what you like with whatever you want. You may, however, find it helpful to avoid coupling full tannic reds with fish; fine expensive wines with strongly flavoured or egg dishes and red wine with puddings.

If drinking several wines with a meal, it pays to move from dry to sweet and from light-bodied to full-bodied. In France you will find that every area has a traditional dish to accompany its regional wine. Often this will be a locally produced cheese, paté or other delicacy. It is here, among the people who made it, that the world's greatest drink can be enjoyed to perfection.

TASTING TALK

One of the most mystifying and frequently satirised elements of the whole business of wine, is the jargon used by "experts". Sagely being told that a wine is "flabby" or "chewy" or "oakey" can baffle or annoy if you don't know what the terms mean, and if you suspect the "expert" of making them up. However, there is a repertoire of terms that most tasters regard as being common and reasonably widely understood.

Acidity: The element in wine that makes it fresh and alive.
Aftertaste: Sensation left in mouth after wine has been spat out or swallowed. Unlike *finish* or *length*, aftertaste can be unpleasant.
Aroma: Simple smell, usually of a young wine. A *bouquet* can be made of several aromas.
Astringent: Harsh sensation/taste that puckers the mouth.
Balance: A balanced wine has all the elements needed in harmony: *fruitiness, acidity, alcohol* and *tannin*.
Bead: Term given to a stream of bubbles in a sparkling wine.
Body: The "weight" of a wine – a full bodied wine will fill the mouth with flavour. Body is closely related to alcoholic content.
Bouquet: The smell of a *complex*, developed wine, made up of several separate *aromas*.
Chewey: A wine high in *tannin* and *body*.
Classy: A wine that stands out above others.
Clean: Simply a wine that tastes "clean". Some wines can alternatively taste dirty!
Cloying: Sweet, sickly flavour or smell that lingers unpleasantly – like the smell of some sweets or cheap scent.
Coarse: Rough tasting, maybe badly made wine. Direct opposite of *classy*.
Complex: A *complex* wine has an intricate and varied mixture of discernible smells and flavours.
Corked: A corked wine is not one that contains particles of broken cork, but one having a musty smell and flavour caused by the cork having been attacked by fungus.

Crisp: A fresh tasting wine that has a good *acidity* level.
Dumb: Having no apparent smell.
Finish: Pleasant taste left in mouth after wine has been swallowed or spat out. Can taste very different from when you first put the wine in your mouth. Not a residual late taste like an *aftertaste*.
Flabby: Lacking in acidity that would otherwise *balance* the wine.
Fruit: Important quality in young wine. Taste coming directly from the grape.
Fruity: Wine in which you can taste a lot of *fruit*.
Full-bodied: Surprisingly, a wine with a lot of *body*.
Gamey: Meaty smell – like that of hung game.
Green: A wine with too much youthful *acidity*.
Hot: Highly alcoholic wine.
Length: A wine is said to have length or be long if it has a good *finish*.
Light: Opposite of *full-bodied*.
Made: A made wine is not vinified from freshly harvested grapes, but a grape concentrate for example.
Nose: More sophisticated way of saying smell.
Oakey: Flavour gained from oak casks – *woody*.
Oxidised: Wine that has spoilt because the air has got in and literally oxidised it.
Palate: More sophisticated way of saying taste.
Powdery: Smell like slightly sweet talcum powder.
Racy: *Crisp* and *lively*.
Soft: Smooth, mellow wine.
Spritz: A slight sparkle.
Stalky: Or even stemmy. Tasting of the stalk rather than the grape.
Steely: Wine with good level of *acidity*.
Structure: A well-*balanced* wine will have a good structure, with all its constituents fitting together harmoniously.
Sulphurous: Wine tasting of bacteria-killing chemical sulphur, which can leave a residue if not rinsed away properly.
Tannic: Wine high in *tannin*.
Tannin: Substance that gives body to both tea and red wine. Important in the ageing of red wine.
Tart: Over acid wine.
Tired: Wine that has passed its best.

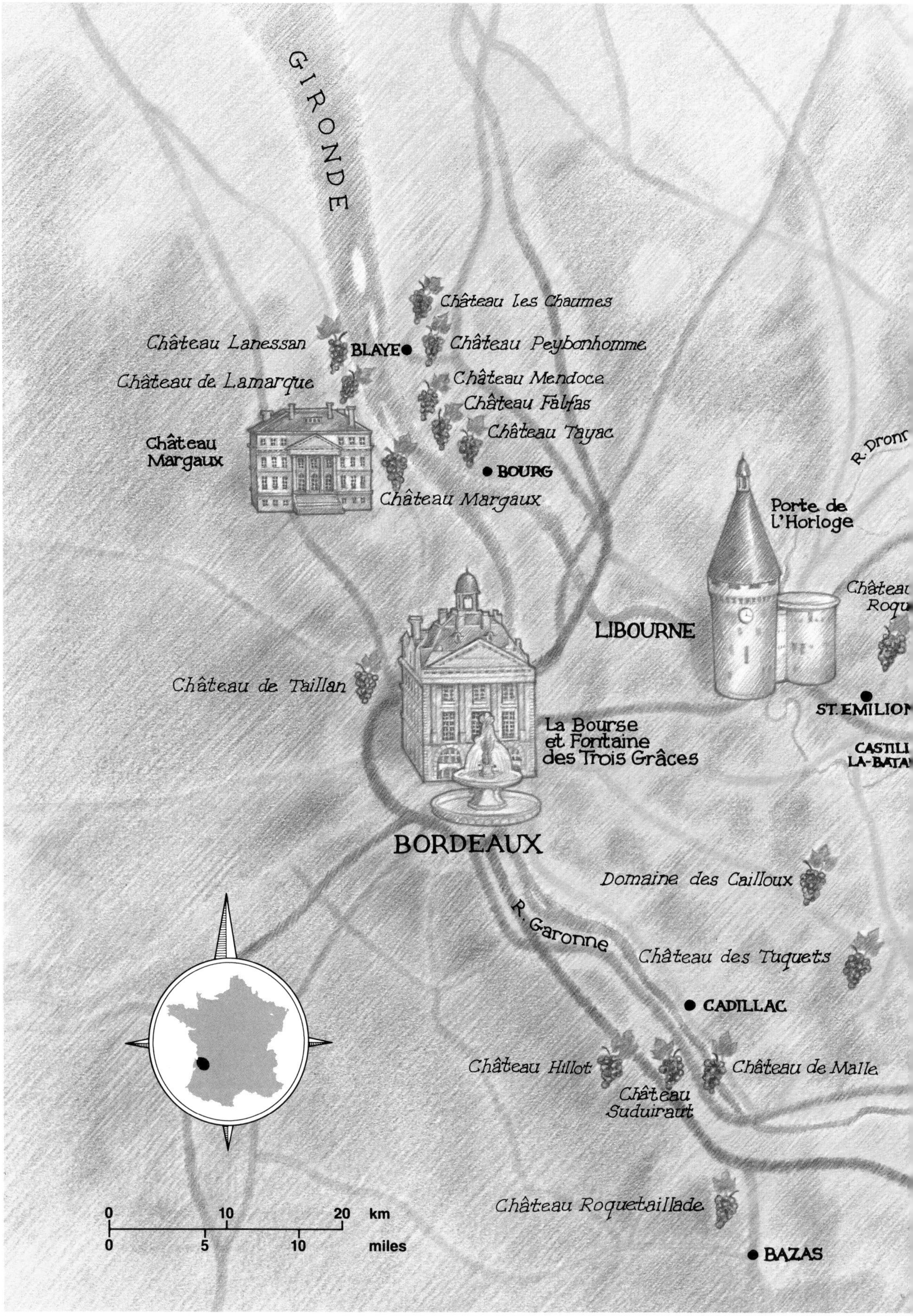

GIRONDE

Château les Chaumes

Château Lanessan   BLAYE●   Château Peybonhomme

Château de Lamarque   Château Mendoce

Château Falfas

Château   Château Tayac
Margaux

● BOURG

Château Margaux

Porte de
L'Horloge

LIBOURNE   Château
Roqu

Château de Taillan

La Bourse   ST. EMILION
et Fontaine
des Trois Grâces   CASTILL
LA-BATAI

BORDEAUX

Domaine des Cailloux

R. Garonne

Château des Tuquets

● CADILLAC

Château Hillot   Château de Malle

Château
Suduiraut

Château Roquetaillade

0   10   20   km
0   5   10   miles

● BAZAS

R. Dronr

R. Isle

STE. FOY-LA-GRANDE

Dordogne

Château de la Vieille Tour

MARMANDE

The
BORDEAUX
REGION

*S*et in the heart of south-west France, Bordeaux offers the richest selection of wines in the world. Their names alone reflect reputations few other vineyards can emulate – from the incomparable clarets of the Médoc, the fine red wines of Saint-Emilion to the sweet whites of Sauternes.

Between the Dordogne and Garonne is the largest of the Bordeaux producing areas, Entre-Deux-Mers. South of the Garonne, to the east of the pine forests of Les Landes you will find the classic sweet white wines of the area.

The city and busy port of Bordeaux, the dowry of Eleanor of Aquitaine when she married Henry II, dominates the region which took its name. To the north are the interesting towns of Bourg and Blaye, the ancient city of Libourne, the ecclesiastical centre of Saint-Emilion, Castillon-la-Bataille on the banks of the Dordogne and Cadillac on the Garonne.

The landscape here is as rich as the wines it produces. From forest to moorland, plateaux, valleys and hillsides, the scenery is a fascinating patchwork created by man and nature together. This provides the ideal setting for the many châteaux, abbeys, churches and prehistoric sites that give a further dimension to this popular region. And to the west, the Atlantic's spectacular sandy coastline awaits the visitor, stretching south to the border with Spain.

The BORDEAUX

REGION

The home of classic wines and once the proud possession of the English, Bordeaux offers much to satisfy the traveller's image of France – good food, good wine, picturesque countryside, superb beaches and a sympathetic climate.

Wherever you travel through Bordeaux, it is hard – almost impossible – to escape from that element which has made the region famous – its vineyards. For in the lush green countryside the vines flourish and the wine flows. Either side of the Gironde estuary that leads to the capital city, vineyards spread like a patchwork across the landscape.

Approaching from the north, through Cognac country, you reach the vineyards of Blaye and Bourg, which follow the right bank of the Gironde. The red wine here is generally of exceptional value, and there are many delightful châteaux of interest, if not quite on the grand scale of those in the Médoc. The citadel at Blaye is worth a visit and from here you can take the ferry across the Lamarque. To the south is Bourg, a small historical town with steep, narrow steps leading down to the river.

Driving south-west, you pass through the vineyards of Fronsac and on to the city of Libourne on the north bank of the Dordogne. From here you are within a few miles of the great ecclesiastical and wine centre of Saint-Emilion, surrounded by fine châteaux and the vines which produce the elegant red wine for which this small area is famous. The hilltop town itself is fascinating and a must for the curious visitor.

South of Saint-Emilion the wine of Entre-Deux-Mers comes from the vineyards at the heart of Bordeaux country between the Dordogne and Garonne. The green, rolling landscape provides many pleasant excursions through woodland, fields of sunflowers and maize and row upon row of vines.

The southern part of this area along the banks of the Garonne, and down to the edge of the mighty pine forests of Les Landes, is the home of Bordeaux sweet wines, centred round Preignac, Barsac and the pleasant village of Sauternes.

Where better to end a trip through Bordeaux than in the Médoc. The road that runs north of the region's capital along the left bank of the Gironde is lined with grand mansions and châteaux. Sadly few of the best known are open to the visitor, but you can admire them from the gateways.

Bordeaux itself is a bustling city of fine grey stone buildings with a magnificent centre, close to the river. Here you can wander for hours, admiring the fine churches, the majestic theatre, the busy squares, shops, restaurants and street cafés. And those who look for other forms of relaxation will find the Atlantic to the west with mile upon mile of golden sand, spectacular dunes and coastal lakes.

REGIONAL SPECIALITIES

The Wines
Médoc: Médoc, Haut-Médoc, Saint-Estèphe, Pauillac, Saint-Julien, Moulis, Listrac, Margaux.
Bourg/Blaye: Côtes de Bourg, Premieres Côtes de Blaye, Côtes de Blaye.
Libourne: Saint-Emilion, Saint-Georges Saint Emilion, Montagne Saint-Emilion, Lussac Saint-Emilion, Puisseguin Saint-Emilion, Pomerol, Lalande de Pomerol, Fronsac, Canon-Fronsac, Bordeaux Supérieur Côtes de Castillon, Bordeaux Supérieur Côtes de Francs.

Entre-Deux-Mers: Bordeaux, Bordeaux Supérieur, Cadillac, Côtes de Bordeaux Saint-Macaire, Entre-Deux-Mers, Graves de Vayres, Loupiac, Premieres Côtes de Bordeaux, Sainte-Croix-du-Mont, Sainte-Foy-Bordeaux.
Sauternes: Cérons, Barsac, Sauternes.
Graves: Graves, Graves Supérieur.

The Food
Steak served with the traditional sauce à la bordelaise, (made with shallots and red wine) is a classic dish. The local fish soup is called chaudrée, and other fish specialities include oysters from Arachon (often served with sausages) and in springtime lampreys from the Gironde in red wine. During the mushroom season, cèpes are delightful.

Left. This elderly lady and her companion make hay while the sun shines, in Saint Christophe des Barges, near Saint Emilion.
Below. Tiled rooftops in Saint Emilion.
Bottom. The Château Loudenne flys the Union Jack alongside the Tricoleur as it has been British-owned since the 1870s.

CHATEAU les CHAUMES

FOURS

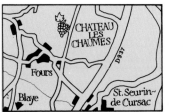

Robert Parmentier is a most interesting and engaging man who has looked after the Château les Chaumes, a few kilometres from Blaye, for more than 20 years. Before that he had produced wine, somewhat further south, in Algeria.

M. Parmentier is justly proud of his estate which ranges from the neatly cultivated rows of vines that surround the property to the château itself. Before M. Parmentier bought les Chaumes, it had been in the hands of the same family – Lapeyre – for more than 150 years. In fact he has the original hand-written accounts and ledger books from 1830 to prove it. He is proud of the château's traditions and rightly strives to maintain them by concentrating on the quality of the wine rather than quantity.

The picking is done by machine and M. Parmentier employs just five people to help look after the vineyard, such is the efficiency of the estate. A further aspect reflecting the insistence on quality is the fact that he keeps the red wine in oak barrels for up to 24 months to allow it to age gracefully.

Château les Chaumes *(Robert Parmentier)*
Fours
33390 Blaye
Telephone: 57 42 18 44

The Château les Chaumes – centrepiece of Robert Parmentier's proudly-kept estate.

CHATEAU PEYBONHOMME

CARS

Making wine is very much a family business for Jacques Bossuet, who owns some of the premier vineyards in the area. The Domaine de Peybonhomme-les-Tours is situated on one of the highest points outside Blaye and dominates the area – not only in terms of its geography but also with its wines.

Yet the success of the wines produced here – and at the adjoining properties of le Thil, Gadeau and la Bigarderie – has not affected that all-important personal approach to the business. This is demonstrated in the welcome and warmth of M. Bossuet and his son-in-law Jean-Luc Hubert.

Dating back several centuries, Peybonhomme has been considerably extended, particularly since 1919, when it passed into the hands of M. Boussuet's grandfather. The

Dominating the area the Château Peybonhomme has been in the Bousset family since 1919.

family looks after 60 hectares of vines in the commune of Cars, Plassac and Blaye and the five wines are produced by traditional methods of vinification. M. Bossuet insists that the *cuvaison* lasts for over three weeks – longer than usual for this process.

The family is happy to show you round the winery, and then you may be shown into a most comfortable and well-equipped *salle de dégustation*. A visit to the Château Peybonhomme is a pleasure you will not quickly forget, for the warmth of its welcome and the interest shown by the Bossuet family.

Château Peybonhomme (*Jacques Bossuet*)
Cars
33390 Blaye
Telephone: 57 42 11 95

CHATEAU MENDOCE

V I L L E N E U V E

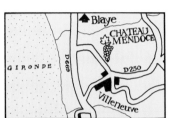

Mendoce must surely be one of the prettiest châteaux in this – or any other – region. Careful restoration has revived the style and elegance of the original property, which had suffered over the centuries from the turmoils that plagued France. The château is set inland a little from the river, on rising ground right on the border of the appellation. And from the first, it is clear the Mendoce is in good hands, thanks to the energy and enthusiasm of its young owner, Philippe Darricarrère.

M. Darricarrère has not always been a *viticulteur,* having trained as a pharmacist. But he loved wine and its production so much that he decided to turn to it as a full-time occupation, following the tradition of his father and grandfather.

At Château Mendoce you can see a perfect blend of the old and the new. There is the château itself, steeped in history that goes back for more than a thousand years. And there is the *vendange*, where people and machines share the responsibility for gathering the precious grapes from the 10 hectares of vines. Three quarters of this goes to make up the Bourgeais red and the rest the white.

Inside the winery, the *cuves* are modern. Yet, again, old and new meet, since the wine is eventually left to age in old oak barrels underground.

Château de Mendoce (*Philippe Darricarrère*)
Villeneuve
33710 Bourg-sur-Gironde
Telephone: 57 42 25 95

Left. *Winery staff hard at work cleaning out the cuves.*
Below. *The Château Mendoce – carefully restored to its former glory.*

CHATEAU FALFAS

BAYON

Maybe not quite as grand as some of the châteaux on the "other" bank of the Gironde, Falfas is nevertheless an imposing sight. It stands proudly on the rising ground above the main road from Bourg to Blaye, overlooking the river and the Médoc beyond. Although the château has enjoyed a mixed history over the 400 years or so since it was built, its future as a producer of fine Bourgeais red wine is certainly assured, thanks to the attentions of Mme Jaubert and her children.

The façade of the château is original, although the building has been added to over the years. Originally, the vineyards that surround the property stretched over some 60 hectares, but today the Jaubert family is happy to harvest the very best of the vines over the remaining 17 hectares. The vineyard has been substantially replanted since the mid seventies, and only a few vines of 50 years old or more still survive.

Although the château itself is not officially open, it is worth phoning to arrange an appointment to visit Falfas, to admire the property, the view and the wine. The elegance of the château is not better reflected than in the welcome of Mme Jaubert, who firmly maintains the traditions that have survived through more than four centuries of sometimes turbulent history.

Château Falfas (*Mme Jaubert*)
Bayon
33710 Bourg-sur-Gironde
Telephone: 57 64 84 04

Château Falfas dates back some 400 years, and is well worth arranging an appointment to visit.

CHATEAU TAYAC

SAINT-SEURIN-de-BOURG

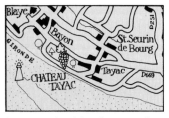

Château Tayac conjures up images of earlier, more glorious times and sends one's imagination back over the centuries of history through which it has survived. The English can lay considerable claim to the early development of the area, since it was the Black Prince, son of Edward III, who sailed up the Gironde in 1356 and annexed Bourg. He even lived for a while in the old tower of Tayac, which is still standing.

The château itself has suffered mixed fortunes over the years, but is now in the caring hands of Pierre Saturny and his family, who have concentrated primarily on renewing and improving the vineyards. The vines cover about 20 hectares and four excellent red wines are produced. You can sample these in the impressive *caveau* adjoining the main *cave*, to the right of the château. Do remember, too, to take a short walk round the other side of the terraces, for here you can appreciate the earlier importance of Tayac, with its splendid position overlooking the Gironde.

Château Tayac (*Pierre Saturny*)
33710 Bourg-sur-Gironde
Telephone: 57 68 40 60

Far left. From Château Tayac's impressive terraces, the visitor can overlook the Gironde.
Left. Foil capsules being added to corked bottles in Château Tayac's winery.

CHATEAU de ROQUES

P U I S S E G U I N

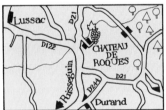

S aint-Emilion attracts visitors like a magnet – and justifiably so. A stroll round the well-preserved streets of this hillside town, surrounded by a patchwork of vineyards and châteaux, takes you quietly back to an earlier age. In fact, vines were planted here as far back as Gallo-Roman times, making the area one of the earliest wine centres in France.

A short distance to the north east is Puisseguin-Saint-Emilion, where you will find one vineyard that should not be missed, particularly by wine historians. The imposing 16th century Château de Roques stands proudly just a few hundred metres from the main road, walled and protected by splendid ironwork railings and gates. It was originally built around 1590, during the reign of Henry IV, and the first owner was Jean de Roques, the French monarch's companion at arms. During the French Revolution, as with so many other aristocratic properties, it was virtually destroyed – save a single tower – and was later extensively renovated.

The present owner is a very personable young man, Michel Sublett, whose grandfather pioneered the re-establishment of the Bordeaux vineyards after phylloxera ravaged the country's vines at the end of the last century.

The showpiece of the château is, without doubt, the Cave de Vieillissement, which lies some 7 metres under the château and covers approximately 800 square metres.

A thriving wine town, vineyards grow right up to Saint-Emilion's old battlement walls.

Here the fine red wine is kept in barrels to mature before being bottled.

Remarkably, the *cave* was only discovered by accident a few years ago. The floor in the château's drawing room was in desperate need of repair and when the boards were lifted, a large hollowed-out area was uncovered. Further investigation revealed a series of passages leading to spacious cellars. The whole area remains at a constant 10° or 11°C, with a high level of humidity. There is plenty of evidence of this, since within weeks mould will start to form round new barrels. The barrels and the walls are permanently covered with mould, giving the whole place a not unpleasant musty smell. Of course, these conditions are absolutely ideal for helping the young red wine to mature.

Apart from the wine, there is an impressive display of artefacts from the wine-making industry of bygone years. There is a number of cooper's tools and such novelties as barrel-cleaning equipment, an ancient wine press and a special branding tool. This was used to burn the name of the château on to the barrels, before the days when the wine was put into bottles and labelled.

Château de Roques *(Michel Sublett)*
Puisseguin
33570 Lussac
Telephone: 57 74 69 56

DOMAINE des CAILLOUX

R O M A G N E

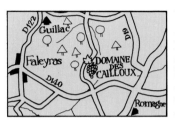

Deep in the appellation of Entre-Deux-Mers the Domaine des Cailloux is an ambitious little vineyard, covering 15 hectares at the time of my visit, but due to expand to 21 hectares in time. This is thanks in part to the hard work and enthusiasm of *propriétaire* Nicole Legrand's son Benoit, and the happy team of workers who look after the estate.

Talking to Benoit, it is easy to be captured by this young man's enthusiasm for wine and its production. He takes his inheritance very seriously – it goes back to his great grand-

Springtime in a well kept Bordeaux vineyard.

father – and discusses the expansion of the *cuves* and the *chai* with relish. However, he is also very conscious of the problems associated with a vineyard that is suffering from earlier neglect and realises that he has a few difficult years ahead.

The *domaine* itself dates back several centuries and was originally attached to the nearby château. It has been extensively renovated and now houses three generations of the Legrand family. The generosity of this lush area of France is well reflected in the welcome that awaits the visitor here.

Domaine des Cailloux
(Mme Nicole Legrand-Dupuy)
Romagne
33760 Targon
Telephone: 56 23 60 17

CHATEAU des TUQUETS

S A I N T - S U L P I C E - d e - P O M M I E R S

Don't be misled by the location – at the Château des Tuquets the emphasis is definitely on wine, not apples. And red wine accounts for two-thirds of the production from the Laville family's 70 hectares of top class vines.

Jean-Hubert Laville is very much in charge of the five châteaux run by the family, which has produced wine in successive generations – father to son – since 1510. Tuquets is the most recent addition, bought in 1976, and is being developed into an ultra-modern winery under the strict supervision of Jean-Hubert.

Apart from Saint-Sulpice, which includes Château Davril, the family owns Château du Mont Carlau at Saint-Felix-de-

Foncaude, Château la Gaborie at Ladaux and Château Lacombe at Gornac. The *vendange* from all the other vineyards is brought to Tuquets to be processed, resulting in no less than 10 different wines.

With all the gleaming modern equipment, representing the future of wine-making, it is encouraging to see rows of oak barrels, proving that not all the traditional ways have been discarded.

When I visited them, they were planning additional facilities, such as new *caves* and a *salle de dégustation*, and also the showing of a video film highlighting a typical year (if there is such a thing) in the life of a winemaker.

Château des Tuquets *(Jean-Hubert Laville)*
Saint-Sulpice-de-Pommiers
33540 Sauveterre-de-Guyenne
Telephone: 56 71 53 56

CHATEAU de la VIEILLE TOUR
S A I N T - M I C H E L - d e - L A P U J A D E

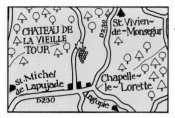

About 150 years have passed since Pierre Boissoneau bought the Château de la Vieille Tour. Although probably little has changed in the small hamlet of Chapelle-Lorette, this family business certainly has. The property has been handed down through successive generations and is at present very much a father and son affair. The present Pierre Boissoneau and son Christian work closely together to guarantee the quality of red wine that is produced from the 20 hectares of Merlot and Cabernet vines. Looking to the future, further expansion of the vineyards and buildings is planned.

The vineyards, incidentally, are the furthest east of all in the appellation of Bordeaux, but provide a substantial outpost for this important wine-producing region.

Château de la Vieille Tour is situated on the hillside above Chapelle-Lorette and commands a fine position in this green and fertile landscape. The property has a well-preserved pigeon tower – very unusual in this part of the

The old pigeon tower from which the Château de la Vielle Tour gains its name.

region – which provides a major attraction as you enter up the drive-in from the road.

Château de la Vieille Tour
(Pierre and Christian Boissonneau)
Saint-Michel de Lapujade
33190 La Réole
Telephone: 56 61 72 14

CHATEAU ROQUETAILLADE
M A Z E R E S

This château's name conjures up images of an ancient fortress, carved in rock, grand in its setting and full of medieval splendour. When you see it you'll realise that Château Roquetaillade is all this and more. There are in fact two châteaux here – the original 12th century Château Vieux and the main Château Neuf, built at the beginning of the 14th century with a considerable amount of English influence.

The history of the place is impressive, with former occupants including a nephew of Pope Clement V, who was made archdeacon at Oxford in recognition of the help given to the English at Aquitaine. Today, the château is one of the most important historical monuments in France, with about 100,000 visitors each year.

The château's vineyards are being re-established by the Vicomte and Vicomtesse de Baritault, who hope to increase the area to 15 hectares by the mid nineties. This will include some land which is on gravel – for red Graves. The production facilities are also to be expanded. And there are plans afoot to add more facilities for visitors to the estate, including a restaurant, a championship golf course and an

Making sure no bucket goes half full to the winery, this vineyard worker starts the pressing a little early.

hotel. There is already a farm museum showing what life was like in the 12th century which is well worth a visit, but essentially Roquetaillade is about the château, its history and its wine.

Nowhere is this clearer than in the 13th century cellar, where Vicomte de Baritault organises special wine-tasting courses. In this vaulted cellar, which is 9 metres deep, the Vicomte has a fascinating private collection of early vintages, going back as far as a 1923 Sauternes.

Château Roquetaillade (*Vicomte de Baritault*)
Mazères
33210 Langon
Telephone: 56 63 24 16

CHATEAU SUDUIRAUT
P R E I G N A C

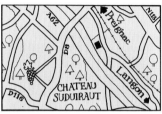

I t will probably come as a delightful surprise to know that, despite the importance of its fine Sauternes wine, Château Suduiraut is happy to open its doors to the serious visitor. The opportunity should not be missed, but do arrange an appointment in advance.

Suduiraut is indeed an imposing sight and the owners, M. and Mme Bachy, are justly proud of both their home and its *vin liquoreux – Premier Cru Classe* in 1855.

In total, some 250 hectares of grapes encircle this 17th century chateau, where the vines are hand-picked, between three and six times a year, to ensure that only the best grapes are harvested at the right time. This means that on average only 12-15 hectolitres of wine are produced per hectare of vineyard.

Château Suduiraut boasts one of the oldest and largest *chai* in the region, with approximately 600 oak barrels laid out in rows the length of the building. These are renewed every three years – the period during which the wine is left to age before being bottled.

There is also a splendid reception and function area alongside the wooden *foudres* (vats). You can view all of

The magnificent approach to the Château Suduirat provides a fine welcome on a crisp autumn morning.

this and the Bachys are happy to let you taste some of their exquisite Sauternes. For those who can't resist the temptation it is, of course, possible to buy from the château.

Château Suduiraut (*M. Bachy*)
Preignac
33210 Langon
Telephone: 56 63 27 29

CHATEAU de MALLE
P R E I G N A C

T here are probably very few better examples of wine production within an historic monument than at Château de Malle – a building which has the unusual distinction of straddling the regions of Sauternes and Graves.

From the moment you arrive at the gates of this classic château, you will be struck by the irrepressible air of the grandeur of days gone by. As you walk up the main steps to the large doors, it is not too hard to imagine the lifestyle of pre-revolution nobility. Today, the Comte and Comtesse de Bournazel have managed to maintain the traditions and

historical interest, as well as the standard of the wine produced here.

Château de Malle has 50 hectares of vines, of which about 20 hectares produce the vintage Sauternes, while the remainder is divided equally between the dry white Sauvignon and the red Graves.

But the visitor's lasting impressions must surely be of the château itself. It has a pretty little chapel, formal terraced Italian gardens with numerous statues, and a curious "theatre" hidden among the trees.

Château de Malle (*Comte de Bournazel*)
Preignac
33210 Langon
Telephone: 56 63 28 67

CHATEAU HILLOT

ILLATS

Traditions die hard at Château Hillot, where Man and Nature appear to have found a way of existing magnanimously side by side, with an obvious degree of mutual respect. At this charming rustic property, just to the north-west of the village of Illats, two generations of the same family can boast nearly 160 years of wine-making. In its own way this little bit of history speaks for itself.

Now in her eighties, Madame Leppert is a formidable yet lovable lady. Don't be misled by appearance, since she is the life and soul of the estate and still takes a close interest

Top. *Château Hillot, seen through its ancient stone gateways.*
Above. *Madame Leppert – the former owner and mother of the current* propriétaire.
Left. *Some of the château's fine vines, thriving in the thin gravelly soil.*

in the château's well-being. Although she has handed over the title of *propriétaire* to her son Bernard, Mme Leppert is still very much aware of what goes on around the estate's 75 hectares. She is justly proud of her country heritage and her château, which was built early in the 18th century, as well as its wines which have won many gold medals over the years. Maybe that's to do with the special, thin gravelly soil, the exceptional care taken over the vinification, the use of Norwegian oak barrels – or possibly just the fact that Mme Leppert walks up and down the vines before the *vendange* to ensure her grapes are just right for picking.

She reluctantly accepts the existence of the latest addition to her very traditional winery – a new temperature con-

troller. Mind you, it does sit outside. A brief shrug of the shoulders and a wave of the hands says it all.

Nothing, however, will alter the charming way in which Mme Leppert relates how in the past people thought much of the size of the *colombière* – the pigeon loft. Apparently the size of a *colombière* indicated the amount of the dowry that the family gave away with a bride. It is left to you to determine how the one at Château Hillot rates.

Château Hillot (*Bernard Leppert*)
Illats
33720 Podensac
Telephone: 56 62 53 38

CHATEAU de TAILLAN

E Y S I N E S

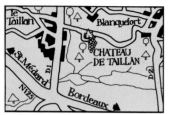

Henri-François Cruse has a problem which is unlikely to be solved. The vineyards of Château de Taillan overlap the border between Médoc and Graves, and since the cave is in Médoc, he cannot sell his white wine as Château de Taillan in Médoc. Similarly, the *cave's* location means that he cannot sell it as Graves. So M. Cruse sells this white wine as Château la Dame Blanche.

Problems apart, M. Cruse owns one of the most attractive properties you are likely to find in any of the wine-growing regions. The château itself, which his grandfather bought in 1896, has remained very much intact and boasts a quite magnificent *cave* which has been designated an historical monument. As you enter what appears to be quite an ordinary winery, you are greeted with the sight of a majestic ballustrade and fireplace, dating back to the 16th century. The fireplace was in fact used to heat the water needed to clean the barrels and other wine-making equipment. M. Cruse can even remember the *Maître du Chai* doing just that in his grandfather's time.

Château de Taillan (*Henri-François Cruse*)
33320 Eysines
Telephone: 56 39 26 04

Because of its unusual situation on the appellation boundaries, Château de Taillan's white wine is sold under the name Château la Dame Blanche.

CHATEAU MARGAUX

M A R G A U X

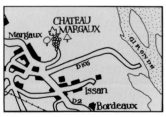

Whether or not you're a connoisseur of wine, it's hard to envisage a trip to Médoc without taking at least a glimpse at Château Margaux. Set in magnificent grounds, at the end of a tree-lined avenue, the château dominates the surrounding countryside along the Gironde. Here, surely is the epitome of the pre-eminence that the great wines of this region have acquired.

Although the sight of Château Margaux should be enough to satisfy the curiosity of the casual visitor, it is possible to arrange a short trip around the *caves* and to see the cooper at work. About a third of the oak barrels used for ageing the wine are made at the château.

The visitor's first view of Château Margaux.

Château Margaux
33460 Margaux
Telephone: 56 88 70 28

CHATEAU de LAMARQUE
L A M A R Q U E

The Fumel family has lived in Château de Lamarque for nearly 150 years. Throughout this time they have produced wine – often of a rare quality. Sadly, parts of the vineyard fell into neglect after the war, but in 1963 about 40 hectares were replanted. Today, from its 80 hectares of vines, the château is able to enjoy a reputation envied by many.

From the moment you turn in through the gateway, situated right in the heart of the village, and drive down the long, tree-lined avenue, you know you are in for a special treat. This is confirmed when you meet the capable and charming Mme d'Every, who will give you all the information you need about the interesting château, the vineyard and its production.

With any luck, you will meet M. Coulary, the *Maître du Chai*, who will proudly tell you about the wine and how it is made. His wife also has a little influence on the running of the château, since she is the *regisseur* (manager) – an unusual position for a woman to hold, apparently.

Château de Lamarque (*M. Gromand d'Evry*)
Lamarque
33460 Margaux
Telephone: 56 58 90 03

Impressively fortified, Château de Lamarque stands surrounded by a weed-filled moat.

CHATEAU LANESSAN
C U S S A C - F O R T - M E D O C

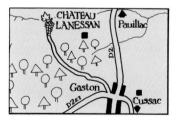

Château Lanessan really began its life as a wine-producing property after it was bought by Jean Delbos in 1793. The family from which it takes its name had originally made their home on that estate in the 14th century.

M. Delbos's son was an enthusiastic *viticulteur*, as well as a lover of horses, and he transformed Château Lanessan into what you can see today. Further property was added in 1933, through marriage, when the family obtained Château Pichon-Longueville (*Grand Cru Classe de Paulliac* in 1855). And in 1961 the family made another acquisition –

Château Lachesnaye.

The 40 hectares or so of the Lanessan vineyard is harvested by hand, after which the fermentation of the red *cépages* lasts about three weeks. The wine is then left to mature in six to seven-year-old oak barrels for up to 30 months.

Visitors are given a guided tour of the winery at Lanessan, where you can view all aspects of production and enjoy a *dégustation* of a variety of wines produced here. There is also a museum of family treasures, including a carriage display and some very well-appointed stables.

Château Lanessan
Cussac-Fort-Médoc
33460 Margaux
Telephone: 56 58 94 80

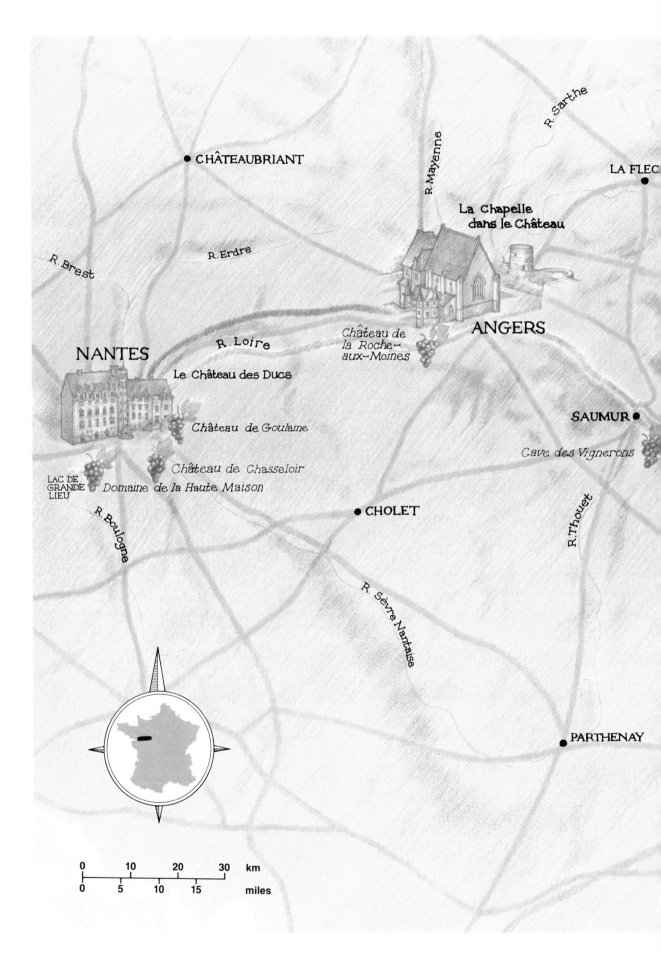

CHÂTEAUBRIANT

LA FLEC

R.Sarthe

R.Mayenne

La Chapelle
dans le Château

R.Erdre

R.Brest

R.Loire

Château de
la Roche-
aux-Moines

ANGERS

NANTES

Le Château des Ducs

Château de Goulaine

SAUMUR

Cave des Vignerons

Château de Chasseloir

LAC DE
GRANDE
LIEU

Domaine de la Haute Maison

R.Boulogne

CHOLET

R.Thouet

R. Sèvre Nantaise

PARTHENAY

0	10	20	30	km
0	5	10	15	miles

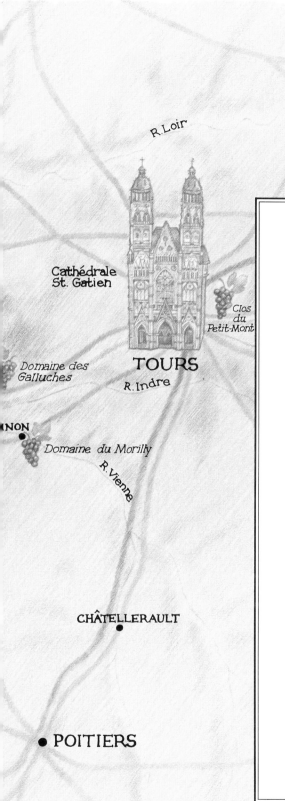

R. Loir

Cathédrale
St. Gatien

Clos
du
Petit-Mont

Domaine des
Galluches

TOURS

R. Indre

NON

Domaine du Morilly

R. Vienne

CHÂTELLERAULT

POITIERS

The
VAL de LOIRE

REGION

The longest river in France, the Loire flows 600 miles from the Massif Central to the Atlantic at Nantes. It is of course château country, a feature for which the region is known throughout the world.

Along the banks of the Loire and its many tributaries there's a further attraction – wine. And this is as varied as the landscape from which it is produced. From the plains around Chartres and the heathland south of Orléans or the wooded and fertile land around Tours (the "garden of France") to the oak forests of Maine and the wetland areas near Nantes, the scenery changes constantly.

The main wine areas are centred round the valley's major towns and cities. There is the predominantly white wine from the vineyards near Tours, the red wine of Chinon and Bourgueil, white and rosé in that part of the Loire round Angers and Saumur and on to the home of Muscadet, to the south and east of Nantes.

Other curiosities include the mushroom caves near Saumur and the vast expanse of inland water – Lac de Grand Lieu – one of the most important areas for water fowl in Europe.

It is not hard to see why this fascinating river was once the playground of the kings of France. And it is easy to understand how they feasted from the culinary delights of this region, particularly the fish, both from the river and the sea, accompanied perhaps by a little Muscadet.

The VAL de LOIRE

REGION

There is so much to see in the Loire Valley, that it is difficult to know where to start. As the area runs almost directly east to west, it makes sense to start either inland east of Bourges or from the Atlantic coast at Nantes. And as the main vineyards are never far from the Loire, the ideal route to follow is along either bank of the river.

Sancerre and Pouilly, well known for their delicious white wines, are situated inland, nearest to the Loire's distant source in the Massif Central. From here you can take the longer route to the west via Orléans, following either the left or right bank, or travel across country towards Tours.

Here you enter the real heart of château country and your trip will be well rewarded by visits to some of the more memorable, such as Chenonceaux on the Cher or Azay-le-Rideau on the Indre, below Tours, before you rejoin the Loire itself. This is the region of the Touraine vineyards – Amboise, Vouvray, Montlouis.

Travelling west along the right bank, the road follows the river and brings you to Bourgueil. From there, moving south and across the Loire you reach Chinon, a popular tourist centre with imposing castle ruins on the cliffs overlooking the town. Chinon is on the river Vienne, which joins the main river just east of Saumur.

The château at Saumur dominates the town and surrounding countryside and from here south and west to Angers are concentrated the vineyards that produce the full range of wines from this part of Val de Loire. Moving on towards Nantes you will find the vines from which the popular Muscadet is made. The vineyards here stretch from the area around Ancenis west and south of the ancient city of Nantes, with its magnificent cathedral and castle. The best of the wine is produced around the Sèvre and Maine tributaries of the Loire towards the fascinating town of Clisson, with its ruined château.

The land throughout the Loire Valley is green and fertile. Flowers abound and fruit grows happily alongside the neat rows of vines. This is no more abundantly obvious than in Touraine – where virtually everything is grown – from apples to apricots, and asparagus to artichokes. And in some of the caves around Angers and Saumur, mushrooms are cultivated. These are well worth a visit to see the massive yield of *champignons de Paris* (the button variety) in the naturally-cooled maze of underground galleries.

Such a fertile area offers ideal grazing for cattle. Poultry, too, is a major source of food. And the mighty Loire and its many tributaries provide another important speciality – fish. Anything from salmon and trout to pike and eel are caught, and all are traditional culinary delights. A whole range of shellfish is gathered from the sea and, of course, there is never any shortage of an ideal accompaniment – in the shape of a glass of chilled Loire wine.

REGIONAL SPECIALITIES

The Wines
Pays Nantais: *Sancerre, Poiuilly Fumé, Muscadet de Sèvre et Maine, Muscadet des Côteaux de la Loire, Muscadet, Gros Plant, Côteaux d'Ancenis.*
Anjou/Saumur: *Anjou, Saumur, Savennières, Anjou Gamay. Côteaux du Layon, Côteaux du Layon Chaume, Bonnezeaux, Quarts de Chaume, Rosé de Loire, Rosé d'Anjou, Cabernet d'Anjou, Saumur Champigny, Sparkling Saumur, Cremant de Loire.*
Touraine: *Chinon, Bourgueil, Saint-Nicholas-de Bourgueil, Touraine, Touraine Amboise, Touraine-Azay-le-Rideaux, Touraine-Mesland, Vouvray, Montlouis.*

The Food
The cuisine along the Loire is as diverse as you would expect from a region this large, with fish and game being among the main specialities. Ranging from the many shellfish found in the west around Nantes, the mighty river also provides the region with perch, salmon and pike – all delicious with a sorrel or beurre blanc sauce. Or you can enjoy a fish stew made with locally caught eels, mushrooms, cream and Vouvray wine. The game terrine (paté) made with thrush, pheasant, quail or hare is a must, as are the rillettes (potted pork or salmon). Typical desserts are pruneaux au Vouvray or poirat du Berry (a pear tart).

Left. The famous Château Chambord standing on the Cosson river east of Blois is a great tourist attraction in the summer. Building of the huge palace was started in 1519 by King François I. 1800 workmen were employed, but it was still unfinished on the King's death.
Below. Fishing in the Loire near Nantes on a summer's evening.
Bottom. Verdant vines east of Bourges, an easy drive from from the Eastern Loire.

The attractive historical town of Amboise. Leonardo da Vinci was one famous resident.

CLOS du PETIT-MONT
V O U V R A Y

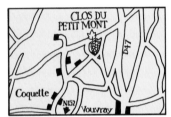

Nowhere will you enjoy tasting the most interesting sweet wine of Vouvray more than at the Clos du Petit-Mont. This small area of vineyards is to the east of Tours, on the north bank of the Loire itself. You will find this small vineyard tucked away towards the head of the valley above the little town of Vouvray. Its vines spread out on either side of the road that winds its way up past the local *cave co-opérative*.

Your host at Clos du Petit-Mont is Daniel Alias, a charming, unassuming man, who runs a very homely, yet successful business with his wife and son. The property has been in the family for four generations, and the vines cover some 10 hectares of the gently rolling hillside.

As you drive through the gates into the courtyard in front of the house, you will notice lemon trees in tubs – a delightful touch and an unusual way to compensate for the lack of a garden. The main wall that fronts the building actually continues round some of the vineyard behind – closing it in and thus giving it the name "Clos".

The cave is at the far side of the courtyard and runs deep into the hillside underneath the vines. It contains a long gallery in which the wine is made, with the *cuves* and the storage vats. Off to the left is a series of passages where bottles of wine are stored and, at the far end, there is a small gallery. Here M. Allias stores some rather special bottles – his personal wine rack with vintages dating back to 1893.

The *dégustation* is in the front room of the house, where you are invited to sit and taste the range of wines produced here. M. Allias will talk you through each one and it is a good time to ask questions, because he certainly knows how to produce some excellent wine.

Clos du Petit-Mont *(Daniel Allias)*
37210 Vouvray-Les-Vins
Telephone: 47 52 74 95

DOMAINE du MORILLY
C H I N O N

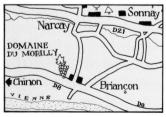

Just a few kilometres to the east of Chinon, you will find the Domaine du Morilly, with its vineyards lying to the north of the picturesque and gently wooded banks of the Vienne, a tributary of the Loire. Five minutes drive from the house is the vineyard's *cave*, where you are most likely to find the *propriétaire*, Abel Dumont. Your trip will certainly be worthwhile, not only for the joy of sipping a wine of refreshing character and simple delight, but also to admire M. Dumont's handywork and to chat awhile – about wine, Chinon, almost anything in fact except the taxman.

The Morilly estate has been in the Dumont family for several generations, and under Abel Dumont's personal ownership since 1949. During this time he has extended both the property and the *cave*. The house, and the design on the wine label, date back to 1877. The building is built of stone quarried from the *cave* itself, and is very much in keeping with the older properties of the Val de Loire.

M. Dumont's great grandfather developed the estate, and ran it as a farm, with cattle grazing and cereal growing alongside the vines. This continued right up to 1949, when Abel took over. Within two years he had expanded the vineyard's share of the estate to around half of the total 40 hectares.

The *cave*, which dates back to the 15th century, was part of a larger quarry hewn out of the steep rocky hillside that runs to the north of the Vienne, and on which the ruined Château of Chinon proudly stands, dominating the skyline above this historic town. Until quite recently the main entrance of the *cave* had been sealed up but M. Dumont re-opened it and cleared away an area inside so that he could bring in the harvest, set up the fermentation, store the wine and then bottle it there. Over the years he has cut away at the rock by hand to extend it and it now stretches to several thousand cubic metres.

Once your eyes have become accustomed to the light inside, you will see rows of old barrels full of the last two vintages, passages lined with bottles and a *dégustation* area lit with candles. Here, you are invited to sit at long oak tables and sample the delights of the wine. The *cave* retains an even, cool temperature throughout the year.

Both M. Dumont and his wife offer the visitor a friendly welcome, and will help in the choice of wine – which you can try either at the house or the *cave*. One of the joys of sampling the wine at the cave is to stand by the barrels while, with loving care and precision, M. Dumont extracts a mouthful or two into the poised glass, using a huge pipette.

Chinon wines are produced using Carbernet Franc stock, which originated from the Bordeaux grapes planted by monks about 1000 years ago. The wines of Chinon can normally be kept for between 10 and 20 years, although in exceptional cases it has been possible to drink the wine after as much as 40 years.

Domaine du Morilly (*Abel Dumont*)
Cravant-les-Coteaux
37500 Chinon
Telephone: 47 93 06 86

The elegant restored 16th century par terres, *low clipped box hedges, in the gardens at Château de Villandry, about 20km west of Tours. The hedges, which are clipped once a year, create a magnificent geometric effect.*

DOMAINE des GALLUCHES
B O U R G U E I L

There's a charm and simplicity about the Domaine des Galluches and its owner Jean Gambier, which are as welcoming as the Bourgueil wine he produces. As you drive into the property along the avenue through the vines, neatly lined with dwarf pine trees, you immediately get the impression of a compact and well-run vineyard.

The business M. Gambier has built up is very much a family effort. His wife Françoise plays an equally important part – even down to organising the *dégustation* in the dimly-lit, atmospheric *caveau*. As you enter this long gallery, you can enjoy some very good wine by candle-light in a small recess to your right. Throughout its length, the gallery is lined with oak barrels, in which the red wine is quietly and graciously matured. At the far end, M. Gambier has his bottle store.

When he's not too busy building extensions to the property or, more importantly, tending the vines, M. Gambier will happily talk about the vineyard, which is 200 years old and has been in the family for four generations. Despite the modern technology employed here, a little foot pressing is still carried out – although M. Gambier is equally proud to show you his special hydraulically-operated *cuves*. Over the last 10 years M. Gambier has doubled the area of vines cultivated at the *domaine* – to 10 hectares.

Domaine des Galuches
(Jean Gambier)
37140 Bourgueil
Telephone: 47 97 72 45

An uncommon sight nowadays – a horse-drawn cart is used to carry grapes back to the winery during the vendange.

CAVE des VIGNERONS
SAINT-CYR-EN-BOURG

You cannot visit Anjou and Saumur without calling at the Caves des Vignerons at Saint-Cyr-en-Bourg. This represents many vineyards of the area, and the explanation of what happens here is quite illuminating.

On arriving, your imagination is hardly likely to be set racing, since you are greeted with a large warehouse-type complex rather than a quaint French vineyard. But it is worth persevering, because a guided tour round the *caves* is an experience not to be missed. The guide will join you in your car – strangely familiar you may think, but offer the front seat nevertheless. Past the main entrance you are diverted into the yard and told to head for the left-hand corner, which to all intents and purposes has just another set of doors. As you approach, you suddenly sight a dark void and, before you know where you are, you have entered what seems like a concrete bunker.

On go the lights and down you drive. The tunnel finally opens out into maze of moss-lined galleries. Having made a brief circuit in the car, you are then invited to get out and wander round these galleries. Some store rows of barrels, while others contain large vats. Then you enter what looks like Aladdin's Cave, stacked with glistening wine bottles.

You are now 25 metres underground, where the grapes are literally dropped down in the presses and then go on to the *cuves*, where they undergo the usual fermentation process. Walk round several more corners and you will come across some of the 4 million bottles which are stored here. These include the sparkling Crémant de Loire, a glorious pinkish-red wine.

There is much to enjoy here and a great amount of interest. For instance, during the war the Germans used the *caves* to store ammunition for their submarine bases at Saint Nazaire, Lorient and la Pallice. They finally tried to blow the place up, but only succeeded in creating a vast fire that burnt for many days.

Caves des Vignerons
Route de Saumoussay
Saint-Cyr-en-Bourg
49260 Montreuil Bellay
Telephone: 41 51 61 09

CHATEAU de la ROCHE-aux-MOINES
S A V E N N I E R E S

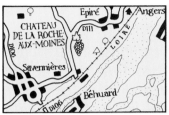

There are many good reasons for visiting the Château de la Roche-aux-Moines. The position of this most elegant vineyard on the north bank of the Loire, just south-west of Angers, is spectacular. And the special dry white wine produced here – Coulée de Serrant – is an equal pleasure.

If you take the second turning into the château, off the Angers road out of Savennières, you will drive past the original 12th century monastery, covered in vines and set picturesquely in the valley that runs up from the river. Whether you drive along beside the cypress-lined avenue that once formed the majestic approach to the château, or prefer to simply walk beneath its shade, you can sense the tranquility and former splendour of the estate. Some of the vines still growing here are more than 100 years old, and the soil is now very strong, since it has been cultivated for more than 700 years.

Such is the gradient of the terrain that the cultivation of the vines is still carried out with horse-drawn implements, and all the grapes are hand-picked by specialist teams of experienced pickers. These skilled workers know exactly which grapes to select – first the best and then the rest! The best grapes from the château's 7 hectares of vines go to make the renowned Coulée de Serrant wine.

All this and more will be explained to the visitor by the charming hostess, Madame Joly, or her son. There is a grace and quality surrounding the château, the estate and the wine that makes this vineyard one of some rarity and necessarily an important part of a visit to the Val de Loire.

Château de la Roche-aux-Moines
(Madame Joly)
49170 Savennières
Telephone: 41 72 22 32

CHATEAU de GOULAINE
H A U T E · G O U L A I N E

Any journey through the Val de Loire would be incomplete without a look at a few of the world-famous châteaux that attract visitors to this area each year. Apart from their style, elegance, historical importance and other points of interest, some are inextricably linked with the story of wine and wine-making in the region.

One such is the Château de Goulaine. Rich in history, the château surprisingly survived the ravages of the peasantry during the Revolution. Today it stands impressively unscathed at the end of a long tree-lined avenue and with a spreading backdrop of the 20 or so hectares of vines which

Above. The salon bleu (blue room) – one of the rooms at the Château de Goulaine that is open to the public. Right. The splendid Château, which survived the ravages of the revolution, is here seen from the air.

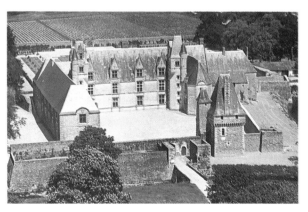

produce the Muscadet Sèvre et Maine. Elsewhere, estate-owned vineyards also produce Gros Plant and the very distinctive Millenaise.

As well as the wines, which you can taste in the reception area as you leave the house, you must remember to take in the château's quite extraordinary collection of live butterflies. Inside a specially heated greenhouse, you can walk among many different and spectacular tropical species – a reward in itself for the visit. Three main rooms are also open to the public, containing various tapestries, paintings and other items of historical interest.

Château de Goulaine (*Marquis de Goulaine*)
Haute-Goulaine
44115 Basse-Goulaine
Telephone: 40 54 91 42

CHATEAU de CHASSELOIR
S A I N T - F I A C R E

It isn't a coincidence that the largest producer of Muscadet Sèvre et Maine centres its operation at the confluence of these two important rivers – important because they define that part of the Nantais region which provides much of the best of this delightfully fresh, dry white wine. The Château de Chasseloir is the most extensive of the properties owned by the Chéreau-Carré family, making up 20 of the 100 or so hectares of their six estates. It is a busy centre of activity, particularly during the *vendange*, but never so much so that the hosts cannot spare the time to give you a generous welcome.

From the ageing vines just outside the château, some of which are over 100 years old, to the modern equipment in which the Muscadet "Nouveau" ferments, a trip around the estate covers a long and full history. Sadly, all that is left of the original 15th century château is a solitary tower. But from this you can gain an excellent view of the immediate area and the Maine, as it flows gently between the wooded banks below the château.

One of the many delightful aspects of Chasseloir is the galleried *cave*, lined with oak barrels. If you look up at the walls, you will see decorative Rabelaisian carvings at the base of each rafter. These denote virtues on one side and

vices on the other, although in these surroundings you may be forgiven for ignoring chastity in favour of gluttony! A further pleasing feature is a line of stained glass

Above. The Château de Chasseloir's galleried cave.
Right. This tower is all that remains of the original 15th century château. It makes an excellent vantage point for views of the vines and river.

windows, which depict the story of the vine and the wine. To complete this wealth of treasures is a selection of traditional wine-making tools.

Although there is no guarantee, if you speak nicely to the warm and friendly host Bernard Chéreau, you may well be able to visit his other property, the Château de Coing. This stands proudly among the trees at the point at which the two rivers meet. Here you can see the underground *cuves* and sample the delicious Muscadet Sur Lis.

Château de Chasseloir
(Madame Edmonde Chéreau)
44690 Saint-Fiacre
Telephone: 40 54 81 15

Another full load for the winery! Work for man and beast in a Loire vineyard during the vendange.

DOMAINE de la HAUTE MAISON
SAINT-AIGNAN de GRAND-LIEU

A visit to Saint-Aignan will most likely take in a look at the Lac de Grand-Lieu. This is one of the largest and most important stretches of inland water in France – if not Europe – for bird life. But you should not leave without calling to see Jean-Nicholas Schaeffer at his charming home.

Entering the courtyard of this creeper-covered 17th century country house, you get an ambience and warmth that is further extended through the bonhomie of M. Schaeffer himself. Here he nobly continues family traditions that have helped maintain the 20 hectares of vines for more than 200 years.

The welcome you receive will last throughout the visit, which takes in a look at the underground *cuves* and some odd-shaped wooden vats. These are traditionally used in the Côtes du Rhône, where M. Schaeffer bought them, although they are in fact made quite nearby in Saint-Fiacre. Finally, you will be shown into the *cave* for some tasting. As you look round you will see a fine collection of wine-making implements on the walls and in the roof space above.

Although M. Schaeffer insists that the Muscadet Sur Lis and the Gros Plant are his main concerns, he will explain that friends persuaded him to produce some red and rosé wines – hence the recent addition of Gamay and Cabernet vines.

Wine is always a pleasure to be shared and the enjoyment of tasting those of the Domaine de la Haute Maison is certainly heightened by the attitude of the host. Sitting in the shade of the trees sampling two-day-old Muscadet – as I did – while eating some home-grown walnuts is a pleasure of its own. Mind you, at such a tender age, the wine is really a little too young.

Domaine de la Haute Maison
(Jean-Nicholas Schaeffer)
44860 Saint-Aignan de Grand-Lieu
Telephone: 40 31 01 83

REGIONAL GUIDE

This regional selection of vineyards has been included to offer the chance of more extensive visits. Phoning in advance will help avoid disappointment. Each wine producing region has a central marketing organisation, normally called a *Comité*

Interprofessionel, from whom lists of vineyards and maps of the often sign-posted wine routes in the area can usually be obtained. Some of the larger wine regions also have a *Maison du Vin* which will provide useful information and often tastings as well.

C O M I T E S

CHAMPAGNE

Comité Interprofessionel du Vin de Champagne
5 Rue Henri Martin
51204 Epernay Cedex
Telephone: 26 54 47 20

ALSACE

Comité Interprofessionel des Vins d'Alsace
12 Avenue de la Foire aux Vins
68003 Colmar Cedex
Telephone: 89 41 06 21

BOURGOGNE

Bourgogne

Federation de Interprofessionel des Vins de Grande Bourgogne
12 Boulevard Bretonnière
21200 Beaune
Telephone: 80 22 67 95

Côte d'Or / Yonne

Comité Interprofessionel de la Côte d'Or et de l'Yonne pour les vins AC de Bourgogne
Rue Henri Dunant
21200 Beaune
Telephone: 80 22 21 35

Bourgogne-Mâcon

Comité Interprofessionel des Vins de Bourgogne et Mâcon
Maison du Tourisme
Avenue du Maréchal de Lattre de Tassigny
71000 Mâcon
Telephone: 85 38 20 15

Beaujolais

Union Interprofessionelle des Vins du Beaujolais
210 Boulevard Vermorel
69400 Villefranche sur Soane
Telephone: 74 65 45 55

SAVOIE & JURA

Savoie

Syndicat Régional des Vins de Savoie
3 Rue du Château
73000 Chambery
Telephone: 79 33 44 16

Jura

Société de Viticulture du Jura
Maison de l'Agriculture
Avenue du 44 RI
39016 Lons le Saunier
Telephone: 84 24 21 07

COTES DU RHONE

Comité Interprofessionel des Vins des Côtes du Rhône
Maison du Tourisme et du Vin
41 Cours Jean Jaurès
84000 Avignon
Telephone: 90 86 47 09

PROVENCE

Comité Interprofessionel des Vins des Côtes de Provence
3 Avenue Jean Jaurès
83460 Les Arcs sur Argens
Telephone: 94 73 33 38

LANGUEDOC-ROUSSILLON

Roussillon

Groupement Interprofessionnel de Promotion des Côtes du Roussillon
19 Avenue de Grande-Bretagne
66000 Perpignan
Telephone: 68 51 31 81

Fitou/Corbières/Minervois

Conseil Interprofessionnel des Vins de Fitou, Corbières et Minervois
R N 113
111200 Lézignan Corbières
Telephone: 68 27 03 64

Minervois

Syndicat du Cru Minervois
Boulevard Blazin
34210 Olonzac
Telephone: 68 43 21 66

Languedoc

Syndicat des Côteaux du Languedoc
BP 1098
Maurin-Lattes
34007 Montpellier Cedex
Telephone: 67 27 84 11

SUD-OUEST

Bergerac

Comité Interprofessionnel des Vins de la Région de Bergerac
2 Place du Docteur Cayla
24100 Bergerac
Telephone: 53 57 12 57

Gaillac

Comité Interprofessionnel des Vins de Gaillac
Maison de la Vigne et du Vin
Abbaye St Michel
81600 Gaillac
Telephone: 63 57 15 40

Cahors

Syndicat Interprofessionnel du Vin de Cahors
Chambre d'Agriculture du Lot
Avenue Jean Jaurès
46001 Cahors
Telephone: 65 22 55 30

Jurançon

Syndicat de Défense des Vins de Jurançon
2 Rue St Ecoles
64110 Jurançon
Telephone: 59 06 53 25

BORDEAUX

Conseil Interprofessionnel du Vin de Bordeaux
1 Cours du XXX Juillet
33000 Bordeaux
Telephone: 56 52 82 82

VAL DE LOIRE

Touraine

Comité Interprofessionnel des Vins de Touraine
19 Square Prosper Mérimée
37000 Tours
Telephone: 47 05 40 01

Anjou/Saumur

Conseil Interprofessionnel des Vins d'Anjou et de Saumur
21 Boulevard Foch
49000 Angers
Telephone: 41 87 62 57

Pays Nantais

Comité Interprofessionnel des Vins d'Origine du Pays Nantais
Maison des Vins – Bellevue
44690 La Haye-Fouassière
Telephone: 40 36 90 10

VINEYARDS

CHAMPAGNE

Château Berat (*J Berat*)
Rue Saint-Roch
Boursault
Telephone: 26 58 42 45

Château Charlier
(*Jacky Charlier*)
4 Rue Pervenches
Montigny-sur-Chatillon
Telephone: 26 58 35 18

Château Charpentier
(*J Charpentier*)
Rue de Reuil
Villers-sur-Chatillon
Telephone: 26 58 05 78

Château Gaillot
(*Gaillot et Fils*)
12 Rue de la Liberté
Mardeuil
Telephone: 26 55 31 42

Château Moreau
Rue du Moulin
Vandières
Telephone: 26 58 01 64

Château Nowack (*B Nowack*)
15 Rue Bailly
Vandières
Telephone: 26 58 02 69

Château Duverger
(*Duverger et Fils*)
15 Rue du Champagne
Moussy
Telephone: 26 54 03 54

Château Frezier
8 Rue Poittevin
Monthelon
Telephone: 26 59 70 16

Château Hostomme
(*Hostomme et Fils*)
5 Rue de l'Allée
Chouilly
Telephone: 26 55 40 79

Château Jacquart
(*A Jacquart*)
6 Avenue de la République
Le Mesnil-sur-Oger
Telephone: 26 57 94 06

**Champagne Moët &
Chandon**
(Service des Visites)
18 Avenue de Champagne
51200 Epernay
Telephone: 26 54 71 11

Château Launois (*B Launois*)
3 Avenue de la République
Le Mesnil-sur-Oger
Telephone: 26 57 50 15

Château Le Brun
(*Le Brun et Fils*)
17 Route d'Epernay
Cuis
Telephone: 26 55 12 35

Château Rocourt (*M Rocourt*)
1 Rue des Zalieux
Le Mesnil-sur-Oger
Telephone: 26 57 94 99

Château Rogue (*M Rogue*)
15 Rue du Général Leclerc
Vertus
Telephone: 26 52 15 68

Château Benard
21 Rue du Corbier
Mareuil-sur-Ay
Telephone: 26 50 60 36

Château Collery
2 Place de la Libération
Ay
Telephone: 26 54 01 20

ALSACE

Cave Vinicole d'Eguisheim
Eguisheim
68420 Herrlisheim
Telephone: 89 41 11 06

**Les Caves Vinicoles de
Bennwihr**
3 Rue de Gaulle
68630 Bennwihr-Mittelwihr
Telephone: 89 47 90 27

**Cave Vinicole de
Beblenheim**
14 Rue de Hoen
68980 Beblenheim
Telephone: 89 47 90 02

J Becker
4 Route d'Ostheim
Zellenberg
68340 Riquewihr
Telephone: 89 47 90 16

Domaine Fernand
Marc Gresser-Kreydenweiss
67140 Barr
Telephone: 88 08 95 83

Armand Gilg et fils
Mittelbergheim
67140 Barr
Telephone: 88 08 92 76

J Paul Seilly
18 Rue Général Gouraud
67210 Obernai
Telephone: 88 95 55 80

Michel Laugel
102 Rue de Gaulle
67520 Marlenheim
Telephone: 88 87 52 20

BOURGOGNE

Maison Joseph Drouhin
7 Rue d'Enfer
21200 Beaune
Telephone: 80 22 06 80

Domaine de l'Hermitage
(*Frères Chanzy*)
Bouzeron
71150 Chagny
Telephone: 85 87 23 69

Les Vignes de la Croix
(*Cave des Vignerons*)
71390 Buxy
Telephone: 85 92 03 03

**Domaine du Château de
Mercey** (*Jacques Berger*)
71150 Chagny
Telephone: 85 87 17 10

Domaine Mathias
Chaintre
71570 La Chapelle-de-Guinchay
Telephone: 85 35 60 67

Domaine Pierre Gelin
21710 Fixin
Telephone: 80 52 45 24

**Jean-Pierre et
Jean-Paul Ragot**
71640 Givry
Telephone: 85 44 35 67

Robert Colinot et Fils
Irancy
89290 Champs-sur-Yonne
Telephone: 86 42 20 76

Chamerose
(*L Menand Père et Fils*)
Mercurey
71640 Givry
Telephone: 85 47 14 14

Robert Ampeau
21190 Meursault
Telephone: 80 21 20 35

Henri Remoriquet
16 Rue de Charmois
21700 Nuits-Saint-Georges
Telephone: 80 61 08 17

Caves Delorme-Meulien
71150 Rully
Telephone: 85 87 10 12

Domaine du Prieuré
(*Armand Monassier*)
71150 Rully
Telephone: 85 87 13 57

Domaine Roux (*Père et Fils*)
Saint-Aubin
21190 Meursault
Telephone: 80 21 32 92

Luc Sorin
89530 Saint-Bris-le-Vineux
Telephone: 86 53 36 87

Domaine Joseph Belland
21590 Santenay
Telephone: 80 20 61 13

Domaine de Chervin
(*Albert Goyard*)
Burgy
71260 Lugny
Telephone: 85 33 22 07

**Château Bonnet Les
Paquelets** (*Pierre Perrachon*)
71570 La Chapelle-de-Guinchay
Telephone: 85 36 70 41

Domaine des Pierres Rouges
(*Marcel Robert et ses Enfants*)
Chasselas
71570 La Chapelle-de-Guinchay
Telephone: 85 35 11 63

Château de Beauregard
(*Jacques Burrier*)
Fuissé
71960 Pierreclos
Telephone: 85 35 60 76

Le Vieux Fleurville
(*Denis Charpy*)
Montbellet
71260 Lugny
Telephone: 85 33 17 14

Domaine La Creuse
(*Pierre Bouthenet et Fils*)
71490 Couches
Telephone: 85 49 63 72

Château de Dracy
(*J de Charette*)
Dracy-les-Couches
71490 Couches
Telephone: 85 49 67 58

Château de Rully
(J de Ternay)
Rully
71150 Chagny
Telephone: 85 87 20 42

BEAUJOLAIS

Pierre Ferraud et Fils
(Yves et Dominique Ferraud)
31 Rue du Maréchal-Foch BP 30
69220 Beleville-sur-Saône
Telephone: 74 66 08 05

La Pisse Vieille
(Jean Lathuiliere)
Cercié
69220 Belleville
Telephone: 74 66 13 23

Les Pillets (Gérard Brisson)
Chemin des Romains
69910 Villié-Morgon
Telephone: 74 04 21 60

Domaine les Rampaux
(René Passot et Fils)
Régnié-Durette
69430 Beaujeu
Telephone: 74 04 35 68

Les Dépôts (Louis Tête)
Saint-Didier-sur-Beaujeu
69430 Beaujeu
Telephone: 74 04 82 27

Le Cellier
(René et Christian Miolane)
Salles-Arbuissonnas
69830 Saint-Georges-de-Reneins
Telephone: 74 67 52 67

SAVOIE & JURA

Savoie

Le Vigneron Savoyard
Apremont
73190 Challes-les-Eaux
Telephone: 79 28 33 23

Louis Magnin
73800 Arbin
Telephone: 79 84 12 12

André Tiollier
73800 Cruet
Telephone: 79 84 30 58

Grande Cave de Crépy
(Louis Sté Mercier et ses enfants)
BP 7
A Loisin 74140 Douvaine
Telephone: 50 94 00 01

Perrier et Fils
73800 Les Marches
Telephone: 79 28 11 45

Château de Saint-André
(Boniface et Fils)
Saint-Andrés-les-Marches
73800 Montmélian
Telephone: 79 28 14 50

Eugène Monin
Vongnes
01350 Culoz
Telephone: 79 81 10 19

Jura

Caveau de Bacchus
(Lucien Aviet)
Montigny Les Arsures
39600 Arbois
Telephone: 84 66 11 02

Caveau en Paradis
(Maurice Chassot)
15 Route de Lyon
39600 Arbois
Telephone: 84 66 15 36

Abbaye de St-Laurent
(Jean-Marie Dole)
Montigny Les Arsures
39600 Arbois
Telephone: 84 66 22 99

Daniel Dugois
Les Arsures
39600 Arbois
Telephone: 84 66 04 31

Jacques Foret
44 Rue de la Faiencerie
39600 Arbois
Telephone: 84 66 11 37

Fruitiere Vinicole de Pupillin
39600 Arbois
Telephone: 84 66 12 88

Les Deux Tonneaux
(Henri Maire)
Place de la Liberté
39600 Arbois
Telephone: 84 66 15 27

Pierre Overnoy
Pupillin
39600 Arbois
Telephone: 84 66 14 60

Désiré Petit & Fils
Pupillin
39600 Arbois
Telephone: 84 66 01 20

André et Mireille Tissot
Montigny Les Arsures
39600 Arbois
Telephone: 84 66 08 27

Jacques Tissot
39 Rue de Courcelles
39600 Arbois
Telephone: 84 66 14 27

COTES DU RHONE

Pierre Barge
Route de Boucharet
69420 Ampuis
Telephone: 74 56 10 80

Georges Vernay
1 Route Nationale
69420 Condrieu
Telephone: 74 59 52 22

André Fumat
Rue des Bouviers
07130 Cornas
Telephone: 75 40 42 84

Domaine des Remezières
Route de Romans
26600 Mercurol
Telephone: 75 07 44 28

Domaine du Roure
(Yves Terrasse)
07700 Saint-Marcel d'Ardeche
Telephone: 75 04 67 67

Les Faures
(Darona et Fils)
07130 Saint-Peray
Telephone: 75 40 34 11

Domaine de Durban
(Leydier et Fils)
84190 Beaumes-de-Venise
Telephone: 90 62 94 26

Domaine du Petit Barbaras
(Feschet et Fils)
26790 Bouchet
Telephone: 75 04 80 02

Domaine les Goubert
(Jean Pierre Cartier)
84190 Gigondas
Telephone: 90 65 86 38

Domaine de Chanabas
(Robert Champ)
84420 Piolenc
Telephone: 90 37 63 59

Domaine le Parandou
(Paul et Denis Grangeon)
Route d'Avignon
84110 Sablet
Telephone: 90 46 90 52

Domaine de la Grand'Ribe
(Abel Sahuc)
Route de Bollène
84290 Sainte-Cecile-les-Vignes
Telephone: 90 30 83 75

Domaine La Fourmone
(Roger Combe et Fils)
Route de Bollène
84190 Vacqueyras
Telephone: 90 65 86 05

Domaine du Gros-Pata
(Garagnon et Fils)
84110 Vaison-La-Romaine
Telephone: 90 36 23 75

Domaine du Moulin
(Denis Vinson)
26110 Vinsobres
Telephone: 75 27 65 59

Domaine de la Janasse
(Aimé Sabon)
Chemin du Moulin
84350 Courthezon
Telephone: 90 70 86 29

Domaine de Grangeneuve
(F et H Martin)
84150 Jonquieres
Telephone: 90 70 62 62

Domaine Palestor La Fagotière (Pierry Chastan)
84100 Orange
Telephone: 90 34 51 81

Château de Bourdines
(Gérard Baroux)
84700 Sorgues
Telephone: 90 39 36 77

Domaine de la Fuzière
(Léo Roussin)
84600 Valreas
Telephone: 90 35 05 15

Domaine Tenon
(Philippe Combe)
84150 Violes
Telephone: 90 70 93 29

Domaine de l'Espigouette
(Edmond Latour)
84150 Violes
Telephone: 90 70 92 55

Domaine de la Rémejeanne
(François Klein)
30200 Cadignac
Telephone: 66 89 69 95

Cave Co-opérative Les Coteaux de Fournès
30210 Fournès
Telephone: 66 37 02 36

Château de Bouchassy
(Robert Degoul et Fils)
30150 Roquemaure
Telephone: 66 50 12 49

Domaine de Roquebrune
(Pierre Rique)
30130 Saint-Alexandre
Telephone: 66 39 27 41

Domaine des Moulins
(André Payan)
30650 Saze
Telephone: 90 31 70 43

Domaine du Vieux Relais
(Félix Roudil)
Rue Fredéric-Mistral
30126 Tavel
Telephone: 66 50 36 52

Domaine de Valsenière
(Bruguier Ducros)
Chemin des Bracoules
30210 Vers Pont du Gard
Telephone: 66 22 85 79

Domaine La Verrière
(Bernard Maubert)
84220 Goult
Telephone: 90 72 20 88

Domaine Champaga
(Philippe d'Olline)
84330 Le Barroux
Telephone: 90 62 33 09

PROVENCE

Château de Mille
(Conrad Pinatel)
84400 Apt
Telephone: 90 74 11 94

L'Arcoise Cave Co-opérative
83460 Les Arcs-sur-Argens
Telephone: 94 73 30 29

Château de la Canorgue
(Jean-Pierre Margan)
84480 Bonnieux
Telephone: 90 75 91 01

Pierre et Paul Bunan
Moulin des Costes et Mas de
la Rouvière
83740 La Cadière-d'Azur
Telephone: 94 98 72 76

Château Vannières
(Mme Colette Boisseaux)
83740 La Cadière-d'Azur
Telephone: 94 29 31 19

Domaine Lafran-Veyrolles
(Mme Claude Jouveferec)
83740 La Cadière-d'Azur
Telephone: 94 98 72 59

Domaine de la Navarre
(Michel de Louvencourt)
83260 La Crau
Telephone: 94 66 73 10

Château de Gairoird
(Comte Deydier de Pierrefeu)
83390 Cuers
Telephone: 94 48 50 60

Château Barbeyrolles
(Régine Sumeire)
83580 Gassin
Telephone: 94 56 33 58

Domaine de la Bernarde
(G Meulnart)
83340 Le Luc
Telephone: 94 73 51 31

Château Simone
(René Rougier)
Meyreuil
13590 Palette
Telephone: 42 28 92 58

Domaine de la Cressonnière
(A M Paganelli)
83790 Pignans
Telephone: 94 48 85 80

Domaine de Grandpré
(Emmanuel Plauchut)
83750 Puget-Ville
Telephone: 94 48 32 16

Domaine la Laidière
(Jules Estienne)
Sainte-Anne-d'Evenos
83330 Le Beausset
Telephone: 94 90 37 07

Château Sainte-Anne
(François Dutheil de la Rochère)
Sainte-Anne-d'Evenos
83330 Le Beausset
Telephone: 94 90 35 40

La Bastide-Blanche
(Louis et Michel Bronzo)
Sainte-Anne-du-Castellet
83330 Le Beausset
Telephone: 94 90 63 20

Domaine de Peissonnel
(Pierre Lemaitre)
83550 Vidauban
Telephone: 94 73 02 96

LANGUEDOC-ROUSSILLON

Languedoc

Château de Grézan
34480 Laurens
Telephone: 67 90 28 23

Château Coujan
(François Guy et Solange Peyre)
34490 Murviel-lès-Béziers
Telephone: 67 37 80 00

Domaine du Combarel
(Henri Bourdel)
34360 Assignan
Telephone: 67 38 04 43

**Château La Condamine
Bertrand**
34230 Paulhan
Telephone: 67 24 46 01

Château Perry
(Geneviève Ponson-Nicot)
Murles
34980 Saint-Gély-du-Fesc
Telephone: 67 84 18 89

Domaine du Temple
(Maurice Muller-Andrada)
Cabrières
34800 Clermont-l'Hérault
Telephone: 67 96 07 98

Château Moujan
11100 Narbonne
Telephone: 68 32 01 25

Château de Fountgraves
34270 Fontanès
Telephone: 67 55 28 94

**Cave Co-opérative de
Saint Drézery**
34160 Saint-Drézery
Telephone: 67 86 95 11

Château de l'Engarran
34880 Lavérune
Telephone: 67 27 60 89

Minervois

Château du Donjon
(M Panis-Mialhe)
Bagnoles
11600 Conques/Orbiel
Telephone: 68 77 18 33

Château Cabezac
(Serge Azais)
Bize-Minervois
11120 Ginestas
Telephone: 68 27 02 57

Domaine Laubre-Farent
(Laurent Fabre)
11120 Ginestas
Telephone: 68 46 26 93

Cella Vinaria
La Livinière
34210 Olonzac
Telephone: 68 43 42 67

Corbières/Fitou

Jean Abelanet
11510 Fitou
Telephone: 68 45 71 93

Château du Roc
(Jacques Bacou)
11700 Montbrun-Corbières
Telephone: 68 43 94 48

**Domaine de la
Voulte-Gasparets**
11200 Boutenac
Telephone: 68 27 07 86

Paul et Louis Colomer
11350 Tuchan
Telephone: 68 45 46 34

Château Les Palais
Saint-Laurent-de-la-Carbrerisse
11220 Lagrasse
Telephone: 68 44 01 63

Château Le Bouis
(Pierre Clement)
11430 Gruissan
Telephone: 68 49 00 18

Château de Vaugelas
Fabrezan
11200 Lézignan-Corbières
Telephone: 68 43 61 20

Domaine de Mandourelle
(Eric Lathan)
Villeseque-les-Corbières
11360 Durban
Telephone: 68 45 90 92

Jean Gauthier-Treilles
11510 Fitou
Telephone: 68 45 71 52

SUD-OUEST

Bergerac

M. Alard
24240 Monbazillac
Telephone: 53 57 30 43

M. Banizette
24230 Nastringues
Telephone: 53 24 77 72

Cave de Bergerac
Boulevard de l'Entrepôt
24100 Bergerac
Telephone: 53 58 32 82

Cave Co-opérative
24240 Monbazillac
Telephone: 53 57 06 38

Domaine de la Truffière
(Yves Feytout)
24240 Monbazillac
Telephone: 53 58 30 23

Château Le Raz
24610 St Meard de Gurson
Telephone: 53 82 48 41

Les Vignobles du Maine
24240 Sigoules
Telephone: 53 58 40 01

Domaine des Templiers
(J R Ley)
24240 St Michel de Montaigne
Telephone: 53 58 63 29

Planque (J de Meslon)
24100 Bergerac
Telephone: 53 58 30 18

Le Marsalet
(Marcel Monbouche)
24100 St Laurent des Vignes
Telephone: 53 57 07 07

M. Unidor
24100 St Laurent des Vignes
Telephone: 53 57 40 44

**Domaine du Haut
Pécharmant**
24100 Bergerac
Telephone: 53 57 29 50

Château Tiregand
Creysse
24100 Bergerac
Telephone: 53 23 21 08

Gaillac

Domaine de Pialentou
(Jean-Louis Ailloud)
81600 Gaillac
Telephone: 63 57 17 99

Château de Frausseilles
(Jean Almon)
Frausseilles
81170 Cordes
Telephone: 63 56 06 28

Mas de Grouze
(Francis Alquier)
81800 Rabastens
Telephone: 63 33 80 70

La Croix des Marchands
(Jean-Marie Bezios)
Le Rivet
Montans
81600 Gaillac
Telephone: 63 57 19 71

Balagès (Felix Candia)
Lagrave
81150 Marssac Sur Tarn
Telephone: 63 57 74 48

**Cave de Vinification de
Labastide de Levis**
R N 88
81600 Gaillac
Telephone: 63 57 01 30

Matens (Thierry Lecomte)
81600 Gaillac
Telephone: 63 57 43 96

Domaine des Très Cantous
(Robert Plageoles)
81140 Cahuzac Sur Vere
Telephone: 63 33 90 40

Domaine Clément Termes
(Jean David & Fils)
Les Fortis
81310 Lisle Sur Tarn
Telephone: 63 57 23 19

Domaine de Moussens
(Alain Monestie)
Cestayrols
81150 Marssac Sur Tarn
Telephone: 63 56 81 66

Domaine des Issards
(Claude Montels)
Amarens
81170 Cordes
Telephone: 63 56 08 03

Les Terrisses
(Joseph Cazottes)
St Laurent
81600 Gaillac
Telephone: 63 57 09 15

Domaine de Gradd
(Etienne Coursieres)
Campagnac
81140 Castelnau de Montmiral
Telephone: 63 33 12 61

Domaine de Bertrand
(Henri Cunnac & Fils)
Donnazac
81170 Cordes
Telephone: 63 56 06 52

Chemin de Balitrands
(Jean-Louis Ribot)
81600 Gaillac
Telephone: 63 57 06 53

Laborie (Jacques Vayssette)
81600 Gaillac
Telephone: 63 57 31 95

Cahors

Fantou (Bernard Aldhuy)
46220 Prayssac
Telephone: 65 30 61 85

Lamarie (Christian Armagnat)
46140 Luzech
Telephone: 65 30 74 24

Triguedina (Baldes et Fils)
46700 Puy L'Evèque
Telephone: 65 21 30 81

Bégoux (Alain Belon)
46000 Cahors
Telephone: 65 35 57 46

Lagérie (Claire Besset)
46700 Puy L'Evèque
Telephone: 65 21 33 94

Les Savarines
(Danielle Biesbrouck)
Trespoux-Rassiels
46090 Cahors
Telephone: 65 35 50 55

Les Cambous
(André Bouloumie)
46220 Prayssac
Telephone: 65 30 61 69

Les Caris
(Raymond Bouysset)
46220 Prayssac
Telephone: 65 30 61 74

Leygues (Robert Burc et Fils)
46700 Puy L'Evèque
Telephone: 65 30 82 07

Domaine de Lavaur
(Renée Delpech)
Soturac
46700 Puy L'Evèque
Telephone: 65 36 56 30

Domaine du Peyrié
(Gilis et Fils)
Soturac
46700 Puy L'Evèque
Telephone: 65 36 57 15

Clos de Gamot
46220 Prayssac
Telephone: 65 22 40 26

Cournou (Jacques Jouves)
St Vincent Rive D'Olt
46140 Luzech
Telephone: 65 20 14 09

La Pouline
(Jean-Luc Lamouroux)
46700 Puy L'Evèque
Telephone: 65 21 30 68

Les Salles
(Roger Lasbouygues)
Villeseque
46090 Cahors
Telephone: 65 36 94 32

Domaine du Souleillou
(Jean-Pierre Raynal)
Douelle
46140 Luzech
Telephone: 65 20 01 88

Matufle *(René Salvador)*
46220 Prayssac
Telephone: 65 22 43 10

Bovila *(Jean-Claude Valiere)*
Fargues
46800 Montcuq
Telephone: 65 36 91 30

Foussal *(Michel Vincens)*
46140 Luzech
Telephone: 65 30 74 78

BORDEAUX
Blaye

Château Les Moines
(Jean et Alain Carreau)
33390 Blaye

Château Loumede
(Yves et Louis Raynaud)
33390 Blaye

**Château La Braulterie
Morisset** *(Jean-Louis David)*
Berson
33390 Blaye

Château Bourdieu
(Jean-Yvon Michaud)
Berson
33390 Blaye

Domaine du Chay
(Guy Beneteau)
Cars
33390 Blaye

Château Pardaillan
Cars
33390 Blaye

Château Les Petits Arnauds
(Georges et J-Marie Carreau)
Cars
33390 Blaye

Château Mayne Guyon
Cars
33390 Blaye

**Château Crusquet de
Lagarcie** *(Philippe de Lagarcie)*
Cars
33390 Blaye

Château Beney
(Henri Bourdillas)
Mazion
33390 Blaye

Château Ricaud
(Michel Baudet)
Plassac
33390 Blaye

Château Chante Alouette
(Georges Lorteaud)
Plassac
33390 Blaye

Château Bellevue Gazin
(Robert Ollivier)
Plassac
33390 Blaye

Château Segonzac
(Micheline Dupuy)
St Genes de Blaye
33390 Blaye

Château Perenne
St Genes de Blaye
33390 Blaye

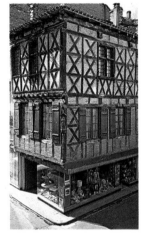

Château La Brousse
(G P et B Broquaire)
St Martin Lacaussade
33390 Blaye

Château Berthenon
(Henri Ponz)
St Paul
33390 Blaye

Château Corps de Loup
(Jean-Pierre Vidal)
Anglade
33390 Blaye

Château Haut Grelot
(Joel Bonneau)
33820 St Ciers sur Gironde

Château Tayat
(Favereaud et Fils)
Cezac
33620 Saint Savin de Blaye

Domaine de la Nouzillette
(Jean-Pierre Catherinaud)
Marcenais
33620 Saint Savin de Blaye

Bourg

Château Beaulieu
(Frank Groneman)
Samonac
33710 Bourg-sur-Gironde
Telephone: 57 68 43 93

Château Bélias
(M. Mexant-Morin)
33710 Saint-Ciers-de-Canesse
Telephone: 57 42 03 25

Château Camponac
(José Rios)
33710 Bourg-sur-Gironde
Telephone: 57 68 40 26

Château Caruel
(Francis Auduteau)
33710 Bourg-sur-Gironde
Telephone: 57 68 43 07

Château Castel La Rose
(Rémy Castel et Fils)
Au Bourg, Villeneuve
33710 Bourg-sur-Gironde
Telephone: 57 64 86 61

Château Croûte Courpon
(Jean-Paul Morin)
33710 Bourg-sur-Gironde
Telephone: 57 68 42 81

Château Eyquem
(Claude Carreau)
Bayon
33710 Bourg-sur-Gironde
Telephone: 57 42 34 40

Château Gros Moulin
(Pierre-Max & Jacques Eymas)
33710 Bourg-sur-Gironde
Telephone: 57 68 41 56

Château Guiraud
(Jérôme Bernard)
Saint-Ciers-de-Canesse
33710 Bourg-sur-Gironde
Telephone: 57 42 32 02

Château Haut Castenet
(Pierre Audouin)
Samonac
33710 Bourg-sur-Gironde
Telephone: 57 42 16 15

Château Haut-Launay
(André Noailles)
Teuillac
33710 Bourg-sur-Gironde
Telephone: 56 42 09 44

Château Haut-Rousset
(Joel Grellies)
Saint-Ciers-de-Canesse
33710 Bourg-sur-Gironde
Telephone: 57 42 17 45

Château La Barde
(Alain Darricarrère)
Tauriac
33710 Bourg-sur-Gironde
Telephone: 57 68 40 66

Château La Croix-Davids
(André Birot)
Lansac
33710 Bourg-sur-Gironde
Telephone: 57 68 40 05

Château de La Grave
(M. Bassereau)
B P No 9
33601 Pessac
Telephone: 57 68 41 49

Château La Tenotte
(M. et Mme Elie)
Berson
33390 Blaye
Telephone: 57 42 05 01

Château Le Breuil
(Henri Doyen)
Bayon
33710 Bourg-sur-Gironde
Telephone: 57 68 42 79

Château Le Sablard
(Jacques Buratti)
Le Rioucreux
33920 Saint-Christoly-de-Blaye
Telephone: 57 42 57 67

Château Les Grands Bertins
(Gérard Dupont)
Teuillac
33710 Bourg-sur-Gironde
Telephone: 57 64 38 00

Château L'Hospital
(Jean Alins)
Saint-Trojan
33710 Bourg-sur-Gironde
Telephone: 57 42 83 60

Château Macay
(Serge Latouche)
Samonac
33710 Bourg-sur-Gironde
Telephone: 57 68 41 50

Château du Moulin Vieux
(Jean-Pierre Gorphe)
Tauriac
33710 Bourg-sur-Gironde
Telephone: 57 68 26 21

Château Peyror
(Michel Jaubert)
Gauriac
33710 Bourg-sur-Gironde
Telephone: 57 64 89 28

Château Rousset
(M.et Mme Teisseire)
Samonac
33710 Bourg-sur-Gironde
Telephone: 57 68 46 34

Château de Thau
(Léopold Schweitzer)
Gauriac
33710 Bourg-sur-Gironde
Telephone: 57 64 80 79

Entre Deux Mers

Château Bellevue La Mongie
(Clément Boyer)
Génissac
Telephone: 57 24 48 43

Château Montlau
(Armand Schuster de Ballwil)
Moulon
Telephone: 57 84 50 71

Château Fonchereau
(Suzanne Vinot-Postry)
Montussan
Telephone: 56 30 96 12

**Château de La
Grande-Chapelle**
(Gérard et Erick Liotard)
Lugon
Telephone: 57 84 41 52

Château Les Tilleuls-de-l'Ouest
(Jean-Gabriel Yon)
Doulezon
Telephone: 57 40 53 72

Château Marac
(Alain Bonville)
Pujols-sur-Dordogne
Telephone: 57 40 53 21

Château Puy Faure
(Bernard Dublaix)
Aubie-et-Espessas
Telephone: 57 43 19 44

Château Timberlay
(Robert Giraud)
Saint-André-de-Cubzac
Telephone: 57 43 01 44

Domaine de Marinier
(Thierry Cotet)
Cezac
Telephone: 57 68 63 13

Domaine Les Ardouins
(Jacques Courpon)
Saint-Vivien-de-Blaye
Telephone: 57 42 52 90

Domaine Loubéjac
(Nicole Molinas)
Saint-Philippe-du-Seignal
Telephone: 57 46 15 68

Château de Ricaud
Loupiac
Telephone: 56 62 97 57

Château La Grave
(Jean-Marie Tinon)
Sainte-Croix-du-Mont
Telephone: 56 63 21 43

Château Dudon
(Jean Merlaut)
Baurech
Telephone: 56 21 31 51

Château Tour-de-Sarrail
(Jean-Pierre Rivère)
Pompignac
Telephone: 56 30 96 47

Château de Lugagnac
(Maurice Bon)
Pellegrue
Telephone: 56 61 30 60

Châteaux Mougneaux
(Jean Bocquet)
Saint-Ferme
Telephone: 56 61 62 02

Château Labatut
(Michel Bouchard)
Saint-Maixant
Telephone: 56 63 25 22

Château Mautret
(Jacques Mouras)
Semens
Telephone: 56 63 50 72

Château Nicot
(Bernard Dubourg)
Escoussans
Telephone: 56 23 93 08

Sauternes

Château de Damis
(Michel Bergey)
Ste-Foy-La-Longue
33490 Saint-Macaire
Telephone: 56 63 71 42

Château La Rame
(M Armand)
Ste-Croix-du-Mont
33410 Cadillac
Telephone: 56 62 01 50

Château La Grave
(J Marie Tinon)
Ste-Croix-du-Mont
33410 Cadillac
Telephone: 56 62 01 65

Château des Ducs d'Epernon
Maison du Vin
33410 Cadillac
Telephone: 56 27 11 38

Clos Bourgelat
(Dominique Lafosse)
Cérons
33720 Podensac
Telephone: 56 27 01 73

Château Gravas
(Mme Maryse Bernard)
Barsac
33720 Podensac
Telephone: 56 27 15 20

Maison du Sauternes
Sauternes
33210 Langon
Telephone: 56 63 60 37

Château Piada *(Jean Lalande)*
Barsac
33720 Podensac
Telephone: 56 27 16 13

Office Viticole de Barsac
Place de la Mairie
Barsac
33720 Podensac
Telephone: 56 27 15 44

Graves

Château La Blancherie
(Françoise Braud)
33650 Labrède
Telephone: 56 20 20 39

Château Lubat
(Bernard Tach)
Saint-Pierre-de-Mons
33210 Langon
Telephone: 56 63 25 07

Château Lafargue
(Jean-Pierre Leymarie)
Martillac
33650 Labrède
Telephone: 56 23 72 30

Château Bonnat-Jeansotte
(Françoise Camus)
Saint-Selve
33650 Labrède
Telephone: 56 20 25 11

Château Le Tuquet
(Paul Ragon)
Beautiran
33640 Portets
Telephone: 56 20 21 23

Château de Chantegrive
(H et F Leveque)
33720 Podensac
Telephone: 56 27 17 38

Domaine du Moulin à Vent
(Paulette et Pierre Labuzan)
Landiras
33720 Podensac
Telephone: 56 62 50 66

Clos Lamaurasse
33210 Langon
Telephone: 56 62 01 41

Médoc

Château Moulin de Ferregrave *(Francis Ducos)*
33590 Saint-Vivien-de-Médoc
Telephone: 56 09 42 37

Château David
(Henry Coutreau)
Vensac
33590 Saint-Vivien-de-Médoc
Telephone: 56 09 44 62

Château La Tour de By
(Marc Pages)
Begadan
33340 Lesparre
Telephone: 56 41 50 03

Château Haut-Garin
(Georges et Gilles Hue)
Prignac-en-Médoc
33340 Lesparre
Telephone: 56 09 00 02

Château La Tour Haut-Caussan *(Philippe Courrian)*
Blaignan
33340 Lesparre
Telephone: 56 09 00 77

Château Coufran
(Eric Miailhe)
St-Seurin-de-Cadourne
33250 Pauillac
Telephone: 56 59 31 02

Maison du Vin de Saint-Estèphe
Saint-Estèphe
33250 Pauillac
Telephone: 56 59 30 59

Château Cos Labory
(Bernard Audoy)
Saint-Estèphe
33250 Pauillac
Telephone: 56 59 30 22

Château de Breuil
(Gérard Germain)
Cissac
33250 Pauillac
Telephone: 56 59 58 22

Château Langoa-Leoville-Barton *(Michel Raoult)*
St-Julien-Beychevelle
33250 Pauillac
Telephone: 56 59 06 05

Château Prieure-Lichine
(Philippe Lahondes)
Cantenac
33460 Margaux
Telephone: 56 88 36 28

Château Peyredon-Lagravette *(Paul Hostein)*
Listrac
33480 Castelnau-de-Médoc
Telephone: 56 58 17 75

Château Chasse-Spleen
(Bernard Grandchamp)
Listrac
33480 Castelnau-de-Médoc
Telephone: 56 58 17 54

Château Tour Carelot
(Christian Braquessac)
Avensan
33480 Castelnau-de-Médoc
Telephone: 56 58 71 39

Château La Tour Carnet
(Mme M-C Pelegrin)
33112 St-Laurent-de-Médoc
Telephone: 56 59 40 13

VAL de LOIRE

Touraine

Le Vieux Chai-Marcé
(Jean-Claude Barbeillon)
Oisly
41700 Contres
Telephone: 47 79 54 57

Les Liards
(Fréres Berger et Fils)
St Martin-le-Beau
37270 Montlouis
Telephone: 47 50 67 36

La Puannerie *(Elie Bouges)*
St-Julien-de-Chedon
41400 Montrichard
Telephone: 47 32 11 87

Vallée de Cousse
(Gilles Champion)
Vernou
37210 Vouvray
Telephone: 47 52 02 38

Jean Chauveau
19 Rue de Tours
St-Martin-le-Beau
37270 Montlouis
Telephone: 47 50 66 97

Domaine des Sablons
(Jacques Delaunay)
Pouille
41110 St-Aignan
Telephone: 47 71 44 25

Le Breuil *(Hubert Denay)*
37400 Amboise
Telephone: 47 57 11 53

La Racauderie *(Benoît Gautie)*
Parçay-Meslay
37210 Vouvray
Telephone: 47 51 30 47

La Tesnière
Pouille
41110 St-Aignan
Telephone: 47 71 45 59

Le Haut Lieu *(Gaston Huet)*
37210 Vouvray
Telephone: 47 52 78 87

La Caillerie *(Daniel Jarry)*
Route de la Vallée Coquette
37210 Vouvray
Telephone: 47 52 78 75

Domaine du Rin du Bois
(Jean-Marie Jousselin)
41230 Soings-en-Sologne
Telephone: 47 98 71 87

La Rochette *(François Leclair)*
Pouille
41110 St-Aignan
Telephone: 47 71 44 02

Guy Mardon
Oisly
41700 Contres
Telephone: 47 79 52 87

Cangé *(Daniel Mosny)*
St-Martin-le-Beau
37270 Montlouis
Telephone: 47 50 61 84

Les Tassins *(Gérard Paumier)*
41110 Seigy
Telephone: 47 75 08 08

Marcel Percereau et Fils
83 Rue de Blois
37400 Limeray
Telephone: 47 30 11 40

Jean-Maurice Raffault
Savigny-en-Veron
37420 Avoine
Telephone: 47 58 42 50

Nitray *(Etienne Saulquin)*
Athée-sur-Cher
37270 Montlouis
Telephone: 47 50 68 04

Vallée de Vaux
Chançay
37210 Vouvray
Telephone: 47 52 93 22

Anjou/Saumur

Domaine de la Gachetière
(Bernard Barré)
49320 Brissac
Telephone: 41 91 25 43

Les Touches-Coutures
(Daniel Belin)
49320 Coutures
Telephone: 41 54 22 26

Domaine des Hautes-Perches
(Christian Papin)
49320 Sainte-Melaine-
sur-Aubance
Telephone: 41 91 15 20

Château de l'Echarderie
(M Laffourcade)
49190 Beaulieu-sur-Layon
Telephone: 41 78 42 14

Domaine de la Soucherie
(Pierre-Yves Tijou)
49190 Beaulieu-sur-Layon
Telephone: 41 78 31 18

Les Saules *(Pierre Aguilas)*
49290 Chaudefonds
Telephone: 41 78 10 68

Le Petit-Val *(Vincent Goizil)*
49380 Chavagnes-les-Eaux
Telephone: 41 54 31 14

Les Erables *(A Bidet)*
66 Grande-Rue
49190 Rablay-sur-Layon
Telephone: 41 78 32 68

Vignoble du Sauveroy
(Francis et Pascal Cailleau)
49190 Saint-Lambert du Lattay
Telephone: 41 78 30 59

Domaine des Maurières
(Fernand Moron)
8 Rue de Périnelle
49190 Saint-Lambert du Lattay
Telephone: 41 78 30 21

**Domaine de la Pierre
Blanche** *(Ogereau Fils)*
44 Rue de la Belle-Angevine
49190 Saint-Lambert du Lattay
Telephone: 41 78 30 53

Domaine de la Petite-Croix
(Alain Denechire)
49380 Thouarcé
Telephone: 41 91 45 00

**Domaine de la Croix-de-
Mission** *(René Renou)*
Place du Champ-de-Foire
Telephone: 41 54 04 05

Domaine de Michoudy
(Cochard et Fils)
49121 Aubigné-Briand
Telephone: 41 59 46 52

Logis du Prieuré
(Jousset et Fils)
49700 Concourson-sur-Layon
Telephone: 41 59 11 22

Domaine des Varinelles
(Claude Deheuiller)
28 Rue du Ruau
49400 Varrains
Telephone: 41 52 90 94

Domaine des Raynières
(J-P et A Rebeilleau)
33 Rue du Ruau
49400 Varrains
Telephone: 41 52 95 17

Château de Brezé
(Comte Bernard de Colbert)
49260 Brezé
Telephone: 41 51 62 06

Château de Montreuil
(M de Thuy)
49260 Montreuil-Bellay
Telephone: 41 52 33 06

Domaine de l'Arche
(Emile Rouleau)
49700 Concourson-sur-Layon
Telephone: 41 59 11 61

Domaine de Beillant
(Jacques Peltier)
49560 Passavant-sur-Layon
Telephone: 41 59 51 32

Domaine des Sanzay
(Paul Sanzay-Legrand)
93 Grande-Rue
49400 Varrains
Telephone: 41 52 91 30

Nantais

Château de l'Oiselinière
(M Aulanier)
44190 Gorges
Telephone: 40 06 91 59

La Loge
(Donatien Bahuaud)
B P No 1
44330 La Chapelle-Heulin
Telephone: 40 06 70 05

Domaine des Dorices
(L Boullault et Fils)
La Touche
44330 Vallet
Telephone: 40 33 95 30

Château de la Jousselinière
(Gilbert Chon)
44450 St-Julien-de-Concelles
Telephone: 40 54 11 08

Château de la Ragotière
(Frères Couillaud)
44330 La Regrippière
Telephone: 40 33 60 56

Château de la Roulière
(René Erraud)
44310 St-Colomban
Telephone: 40 05 80 24

Château de la Mercredière
(Frères Futeul)
Le Pallet B P 39
44690 La Haye-Fouassière
Telephone: 40 54 80 10

Château la Noë
(Comte de Malestroit)
44330 Vallet
Telephone: 40 33 92 72

Domaine de l'Hyvernière
(Marcel Sautejeau)
44330 Le Pallet
Telephone: 40 06 73 83

INDEX

Acknowledgments

The author would like to thank the following for the help and encouragement they gave to make this guide possible:

John Booth for his valuable research and photographs on Bourgogne, Jura and Savoie.
Charlotte Moremon and Catherine Manac'h, Food and Wine from France (London).
Jean Terrieux, French Government Tourist Office (London).
Nick Stevens, Sealink British Ferries.
The regional wine organisations and their staff throughout France.
Robert Butler, who helped brush up my French!
Jenny Rylah, for painstaking hours typing both English and French.
And of course the many *vignerons* I visited, for their marvellous hospitality and generosity.

Illustrations

Main illustrated maps by Jane Launchbury.
All other illustrations by Fran Stevens/The Design Shop.

Photographs

Michael Busselle Pages 9 (top), 19 (top), 29 (bottom), 43 (top), 61 (bottom left), 66-67, 71 (bottom), 83 (bottom left), 86 (bottom), 91, 97 (top left), 103 (bottom), 111, 112.
Champagne Bureau Pages 9 (bottom left), 11 (bottom).
Conseil Interprofessionnel des Vins de la Region de Bergerac Pages 84, 85.
Eric Crichton/Bruce Coleman Cover, page 5.
Cru Minervois Page 121.
Dr. John Feltwell/Wildlife Matters Page 36.
Food and Wine from France Pages 32 (bottom right), 57 (bottom right), 71 (top left), 76 (top), 101, 102, 114, 117, 119, 121, 124, 125.
French Government Tourist Office Pages 19, 29 (top left), 31 (bottom), 35 (left), 43, 45 (top), 46 (bottom), 53, 55 (top left) 61 (bottom), 71 (top right), 79 (top), 83 (bottom right), 90 (bottom), 97 (top right), 113, 122, 123.
Anne Hughes-Gilbey Pages 29 (top right), 44 (bottom), 47 (left), 72 (bottom), 88.
International Distillers and Vintners Page 97 (bottom).
Le Marquis de Goulaine Page 115.
Moët & Chandon Pages 9 (bottom right), 10 (top), 14 (bottom).

All other photographs taken by the author.